Learn to Think Using Riddles, Brain Teasers, and Wordplay:

Develop a Quick Wit, Think More Creatively and Cleverly, and Train your Problem-Solving instincts

By Patrick King
Social Interaction and Conversation Coach
at www.PatrickKingConsulting.com

Table of Contents

Chapter 1. "I'm a Puzzle that Everyone Loves not Being Able to Solve—What Am I?"

The answer: A riddle!

Everyone loves a good riddle. A riddle is a little hard to define, but we all know one when we see it: it's typically a phrase or question that has some veiled or double meaning and which forces us to think really carefully about the answer. Riddles may seem like nothing more than child's play (the last time you answered one may have been in childhood!), but riddles have a long and illustrious past.

Riddles are a "universal art" found in all cultures, and have been studied by linguists, anthropologists, theologists, and more to understand how and why human beings use these peculiar tales, questions, or puzzles. Want some proof? Here is a riddle mentioned in Greek antiquity, in other words, over two thousand years ago: Ares sent the Sphinx from her <u>Aethiopian</u> homeland (the Greeks always remembered the foreign origin of the Sphinx) to Thebes in Greece where she asked all passersby the most famous riddle in history: "Which creature has one voice and yet becomes four-footed and two-footed and three-footed?"

She strangled and devoured anyone who could not answer. Oedipus solved the riddle by answering: "Man—who crawls on all fours as a baby, then walks on two feet as an adult, and then uses a walking stick in old age." By some accounts (but much more rarely), there was a second riddle: "There are two sisters: one gives birth to the other, and she, in turn, gives birth to the first. Who are the two sisters?" The answer is "day and night." (Both words—ἡμέρα and νύξ, respectively—are feminine in Ancient Greek).

Riddles seem to play with the flexible boundaries of language, showing us the intellectual conventions we didn't even know we were using. Riddles lay bare our ordinary assumptions about the way the world works—and show us that things are not quite as they seem. They provide moments of surprise, shock, and even dumbfoundedness. They make us feel that we are not as bright as we would like to be, and that we are blind to the obvious.

On hearing the answer, we get a flash of insight and understanding, a little joke for the mind that's like the equivalent of an optical illusion or an object that seems to change color completely when tilted in the light. Over time, riddles became a way of relating to others, and even the basis for philosophical questions, thought experiments, and methods of understanding the world around us. Riddles are more than simple wordplay, as this book will demonstrate, and can be used as tools for a range of purposes.

In this book, we'll be exploring riddles for a few reasons, not least of which because they're fun! Riddles can also be thought of as mini exercises for the conceptual mind, and a way to develop critical thinking and analytical skills, as well as strengthen the ability to think creatively.

"Out of the box" thinking may feel random and spontaneous in the moment, but in the chapters that follow, we'll see how there are actually predictable formulas and techniques that can help us solve problems at a higher level than we're used to. Riddles are a brilliant way to practice and learn about these different ways of thinking, if we know how to use them. You can read all you want about different types of thinking—it's an important piece of the puzzle—but if you never apply them in a significant way, then all that knowledge will be for naught.

So first, let's consider the mental tools we have at our disposal when approaching the task that is a riddle. In reality, this is about evaluating the problems and novel situations in our lives, and gaining better understanding and methods to navigate them effectively, quickly, and strategically.

Thinking Modalities

People seldom think of *thinking* as something they need to practice, develop, or strengthen. It's almost as though we assume this skill is a given, and something that will run more or less on its own. Most of us are more focused on developing skills and what could be called crystallized intelligence—essentially knowledge and information. But can we develop muscles in the body without exercise? Can we use any tool at all without first understanding how best to use that tool? What can we actually do with the tool by itself, and no type of instruction manual for best practices?

This is how the vast majority navigate the world. But we can do better than that.

Thinking is an aptitude that is more fluid than we think—and more prone to bias, misconception, lazy assumption, shortcuts, weak hypotheses, and plain old habit. Realizing that your brain can (and should) be used to its full potential is like suddenly discovering that all along you've been using a precious and sophisticated piece of technology as a doorstop. Our brains can do so much more, but we have to deliberately give ourselves the opportunity to consider how we're thinking in the first place, and then dedicate the time to improving it. Let's take a look at some of the tools that will be in our arsenal at the end of this book.

Going Outside the Box

What do you know about creativity? Do you imagine that it's something a bit like a flash of light from nowhere, something that only the rare gifted person has access to? Perhaps you think it's a "left brain versus right brain" phenomena and that some people are just born better able to create and think up new ideas.

We'll abandon these conventional ideas for one reason: they're limiting and limited. Instead, we'll look at creativity with curiosity and try to understand what it *is*. What is a creative person actually doing when they bring something completely new into the world? In understanding the function and nature of creativity, we can then learn to practice it ourselves (more on this later, when we explore riddles). In time, we will be able to systematically become more creative. It sounds like an oxymoron, but most things in this world can be trained and cultivated, and very few things are dependent on raw talent and luck.

Divergent thinking is the name given to the kind of intellectual activity that explores and expands on as many solutions or alternatives as possible. Quick—think of a simple iron nail. How many uses can you think of for a single iron nail? The activity that your brain engages in to do this is called divergent thinking.

Being flexible and open, the idea is to "brainstorm" and open the field right up. This kind of thinking, crucially, needs to be removed from goal-oriented, *convergent thinking*—it works best when you suspend judgment (i.e. telling yourself, "that's a stupid idea") and simply let ideas flow as they will. This is the kind of opening-up, rather than narrowing-down, kind of thinking.

The type of thinking to solve riddles is, you guessed it, almost purely divergent. When three of the most obvious descriptions of assumptions fail, where do you go from there? You must start to think outside your conventional boundaries and diverge. Without it, you will be running your head into the same wall repeatedly.

Lateral thinking is also a term you may be familiar with. In contrast to "vertical thinking," which is step by step and rather predictable, lateral thinking seems to take a step to the side, into a new dimension. It makes you ask how you get from Point A to Point B, and attempts to detach from the current scenario. Lateral thinking is the act of mentally manipulating factors and situations.

We'll see plenty of examples of lateral thinking in the riddles that follow later in the book, and it's this kind of thinking that is best for problem solving or generating truly novel ideas. Imagine a classic maze printed on a piece of paper, with an IN and an OUT. You're given a pencil and told to solve it. You might go about drawing a line from IN to OUT, winding along the paths of the maze.

Or, if you were thinking laterally, you might simply draw a long line *outside* the maze, bypassing the entire thing—you've still solved the puzzle, only not on its own terms. In doing so, you've found the solution at a different level of thinking than the problem was created. Going even further, you could solve the problem in an even more outlandish way: by curling the paper in on itself, you can bring the IN to the OUT in three dimensional space, allowing your pencil to make the tiny jump from one to the other.

You've solved the problem again, by now completely breaking the rules of both previous solutions (you might then pull a *Matrix*-style trick and claim, as your final solution, that "there is no paper"). The point of this thought exercise is to expand your mind and imagine "what if" rules didn't exist.

Systems thinking is similar in that it is the ability to see and comprehend the "bigger picture"—as well as how all its components fit inside it. Understanding large-scale interrelations is sometimes enough to solve a problem creatively.

Connecting the dots, synthesizing separate ideas, seeing the whole, and perceiving relationships and connections are invaluable for those problems in life that are "greater than the sum of their parts"— i.e., most of them! As an example, you may be dealing with a difficult person and unsure how to get them to see your point of view. But really, you can fix things by seeing *their* point of view. When you understand who their boss is, what their objectives and motivations are, and all the complex links that connect you to them, you can better understand their position—to your benefit.

By zooming out, you add context and dimension to the situation, and act accordingly. Many of us have the problem of getting caught in the weeds—for another analogy, not being able to see the forest through the trees. Systems thinking implores you to see the clues and hints that inevitability exist in every situation, and expand on what they could mean for you. It may not appear to be a type of creative thinking at first glance, but if it's something that forces a different perspective, it counts!

Finally, *inspirational thinking* is also a kind of creative thinking, and can be best described as receiving insight or inspiration from somewhere else entirely. Take an entirely different activity, mindset, discipline, or field, and force-apply this to your current situation. For instance, generating ideas that must start with each letter of the alphabet. This gives you twenty-six ideas, as well as fitting an intentional constraint.

This results in a sudden explosion of understanding or a peak experience—a lightbulb switching on in your head. It can seem like this flash of creative insight is unpredictable (a freebie from the mythical muses?), but people who have these insights often lay extensive groundwork and actively court those insights one way or another.

Salvador Dali, for example, was known to drift off to sleep with a spoon deliberately held loosely in his hand, balanced above a china plate. As he began to dream, his grip would loosen and he'd drop the spoon; the clattering on the plate would wake him up instantly. He'd then reach for his notepad nearby and scribble down all the images that had come to his half-awake mind. He called this chasing hypnagogic sleep, as he wanted to play in the area of consciousness between waking and sleep.

In a similar way, August Kekule is reported to have had a dream about a snake biting its own tail, and in a flash, understood the ring-like structure of the benzene molecule—a puzzle that had filled his waking hours. Others receive this inspiration from altered states of consciousness (like dreams), mystical experiences, or even profound moments during meditation or time spent in nature.

We can access this state by simply stepping away from the problem at times and letting our unconscious mind do the work for us. The more varied and different your experiences are, the more mental models you can try on for size and apply to different situations.

Mastering Critical Thinking

Creativity and divergent thinking can be thought of as simultaneously subtypes and examples of one another, wherein the mind goes from a small, narrow, or limited perspective and opens up. This requires different types of frameworks to not be stuck in a box of our own creation.

Convergent thinking, on the other hand, goes the other direction and takes many strains of thought and ideas and boils them down to a narrower conclusion or solution. It's finding a way *inside* the given rules rather than breaking them or seeking new rules and *outside* solutions. Insight comes from digging deeper rather than looking elsewhere.

This is a process of further understanding a narrower set of information and then attempting to draw conclusions from it via analysis and insight. These are both ways of problem solving, which is the true skill that riddles help us cultivate. Whether you go broader or more specific, it's clear that our mental status quo can't quite cut it.

The first thing to remember is that critical (step by step) thinking is not really all that separate from non-linear, insightful, or creative thinking. In fact, the two often go hand in hand, solving one another's unfinished business. In developing all aspects of cognition, we equip ourselves with more tools to use on any problem or situation we're faced with. We can expand in one moment (gathering data, exploring arguments, and taking in the general logic of a problem) before narrowing down again (drawing conclusions and fashioning a single solution). Either way, we are challenging ourselves and using different perspectives.

No style of thinking is better than the other—rather, it's knowing which is most appropriate to use in each situation. Questions like, "What is the atomic weight of magnesium?" require a different kind of thinking than do more open-ended questions like, "How are we going to get our sales team to cooperate more in the office?" For some problems, you need as many answers as possible (or, there is no "right" answer), but for others, you really want to hone in on the single best solution. Riddles force you to alternate between them.

Critical thinking is broadly convergent instead of divergent—it seeks to whittle down, to find logical coherence, and to unpick the components of a problem in the same way you'd take apart an appliance. Though creativity is a kind of intelligence, and intelligent people are invariably deeply creative thinkers, it is critical thinking that's most often regarded as *thinking* in general. People who wish to bolster their intelligence often train their analytical skills. We can ask the same question here as we did above. What are people actually doing when they think intelligently and logically about a problem?

The first step is usually *identification*. Actually seeing and acknowledging what the problem is, diagnosing the issue, and finding all the aspects influencing it. You can never provide adequate solutions if you don't understand the problem sufficiently.

During this stage, you might ask questions like, what am I really looking at here? What's the question/problem? Who are the actors and what are they doing? And why? Can I identify cause and effect relationships here? What am I trying to achieve, and what information am I missing? And so on.

The next step entails a little *research*. Once you've broadly identified the field in which your problem is taking place, you can begin to explore various options, arguments, or possible solutions. Look at information and consider its quality.

Verify your sources and independently look at arguments to see how persuasive they are, and how they're making that argument. Evaluate different possibilities with an eye to a solution. These research skills are invaluable in making sure that you're not using faulty assumptions or bad data to come to your conclusions. A great critical thinking skill is to routinely ask, "What do I think and why do I think this?"

What's the evidence? You could also deliberately search for the opposing argument to counter your own unconscious bias. Rather than merely look for data that supports your already-held conclusions, it can help to ask yourself what you are *not* seeing! This is a step that most people don't make it to, so if you're getting to this stage, you're already significantly ahead of the pack.

This leads naturally to the next step (although all these functions typically overlap): "identifying bias." This requires something we don't often acknowledge when we think of intelligence—the ability to be discerning. Information needs to be appraised as neutrally and objectively as possible. To do this requires humility, honesty, and a lot of maturity—plus a little creative thinking to look into your own blind spots!

Debate with yourself. Find the flaws, weak points, and assumptions in how you're thinking. Actively take an opposing view to understand your own flaws and potential weak points. Challenge yourself to find evidence for your beliefs and assumptions—and be ready to abandon those that are genuinely incorrect. This is the only way learning can ever happen! The worst thing you can do is assume that you are correct, and that there are elements of your thinking that are infallible and not worthy of testing.

This aspect of critical thinking is perhaps more important than any raw, intellectual power—because even the best arguments and most useful information will be ignored if too much ego is involved, or if someone has simply failed to consider all the facts at hand. Our world is overflowing with information, but not all of it is high quality. Yes, that even includes some of yours. If you find yourself resisting a question or assertion, take a second to pause and ask yourself if you are truly dedicated to finding the truth of the matter, or simply defending something else (like your ego).

We need to consistently ask who is presenting the information, and why (what is their agenda and how do they benefit from these claims?). Is it logical, relevant, incomplete, up to date? This may not seem immediately applicable when it comes to riddles, but many riddles do in fact trick us when we fail to properly appraise the problem, or fully consider the nature and quality of the information presented to us.

Inference or the closely related *deduction*, is the act of arriving at a conclusion given the information, or premises, in front of you. This is a process of extrapolation—guessing at some unknown piece of information based on known pieces of information.

For example, if you discovered that someone hadn't worked for twenty years, you may infer that their unemployment was unfortunate and maybe due to some sort of disability (in this example, you can see that inferences can be incorrect—the person may well be independently wealthy, or someone like a monk or nun who doesn't work at all). An inference is an educated guess, but it's still just a guess and is only as good as the premises it's based on.

More specifically, a deduction (in the classic philosophical sense, at least) is used when there is no possibility of the conclusion being wrong, given the premises. For example, I can have the following: "All students scoring below fifty percent fail the test," as well as, "This student has obtained forty-two percent." Using deduction, I can make the conclusion, "This student has failed the test." I have moved from a general principle to a special case.

Deduction of this kind is rarer in real life than general inference—but sometimes mistakes can be avoided by simply knowing which one you're actually dealing with! Induction, the opposite, is more informal logic and moves from a specific case to a general principle. For example, "The sun rose yesterday and it rose today as well. It will *probably* rise tomorrow, too."

To improve inferential thinking, you need only improve the quality of the information you're basing your conclusions on. Many of the riddles we'll look at are deliberate tricks in that they withhold a crucial piece of information that's *needed* to come to the right conclusion. Clues are always useful in critical thinking—but always remember that they're just that, clues.

Another aspect of critical thinking is *determining relevance*. All the above steps assume that you're only considering information that is actually pertinent to the situation at hand. This in itself requires some skill. How do you know when to stop looking, or whether a piece of data is worth including in your analysis? You don't want to get sidetracked with totally irrelevant data, but you also don't want to miss out on crucial information.

The best approach is to have a goal in mind and constantly measure new information against this goal—with many goals, you might need to rank them in order of importance. When you find yourself encountering repeated data, it's a sign you've thoroughly explored the space, but you may have to be satisfied with enough information to merely allow you to identify trends. Like biases, information should constantly be checked for its value in the bigger picture—can you omit a dozen weak ideas in favor of a single better and more representative one?

Finally, *curiosity* is a vital but sometimes overlooked part of critical thinking. The truth is, information seldom comes to find us and present itself perfectly formed! Rather, it is us who has to go and seek it out deliberately, sometimes asking, "Why?" many times over to get to the crux of an issue. It's easy to lose the curiosity habit and take things at face value, but sometimes the best critical thinking is done when people are not satisfied with the standard answer. Critical thinking is solutions-oriented and convergent, but that doesn't mean you can't regularly ask yourself, "Is this all there is?" and go poking around until something catches your interest. Keep things open-ended—at the end of every solution, you often find three more interesting problems!

Putting it All Together

Having outlined a general vocabulary for the different kinds of thinking, however, isn't quite the same as knowing how and when to use these different cognitive "modes" or techniques. When you are out there in the real world, solving real problems as they emerge, you will use a blend of all the above. To become a better thinker, then, takes not only familiarity with the nuts and bolts of thinking, but practical awareness of how to use those skills synergistically in the moment.

This is something that author Warren Berger thought about a lot, and is behind the method he outlines in his book *A More Beautiful Question*. His idea is that the quality and breadth of our knowledge about the world comes down in large part to the quality and depth of the questions we pose to it. By learning to ask better questions (in a more formal and deliberate process), we give ourselves deeper access to knowledge and insight.

Good questions are the fundamental basis of the scientific method in general. By doing science, we ask, in many complex and varied ways, "If I do this, what happens?" Berge's model suggests three steps or stages, and is useful because it combines many of the skills we've explored in the previous section.

To ask truly innovative questions, we should structure them as: Why, What If, and How. Each requires a different mindset, but all three work together for maximum effectiveness. The three questions give us time to switch tools, try on different thinking modes, and give ourselves a better chance at arriving at a comprehensive and intelligent solution.

Let's begin where all interesting things begin—with *Why?*

This plunges us into the world of understanding. Why is the situation as it is? Why this way and not some other way? You can even ask why the question or problem has been formulated in the way it has, or why we are asking the question in the first place. Every problem-solving attempt must start from the beginning. You need to understand why things are as they are if you have a hope of changing them into something else! Asking why also gives you permission to see if things are in fact wrong or could be improved on. You open the door for something else (hello again, creative thinking!).

We don't need to be rebels or contrarians to constantly ask why of the world. Merely adopting a curious stance in the face of the ordinary and expected shows our willingness to engage and understand at a deeper level. By asking why we peek under the hood and examine our assumptions, beliefs, shortcuts, unspoken desires, and blind spots. For example, the sales team is experiencing friction, and bad office politics is beginning to undermine productivity. You could ask:

Why exactly is everyone unhappy?

Why is this now suddenly a problem but wasn't a month ago?

Why have previous attempts to fix the problem failed?

Why do we have the sales team all in one office anyway?

By using "why," we shine a light on all the cause-and-effect relationships in every nook and cranny of the problem. We use identification, curiosity, inference, research, and curiosity to feel the problem out. This will come especially handy when trying to solve riddles that are carefully worded and presented. But in truth, this same process occurs in everyday life.

Next, we open up further and ask, *What if?*

Now we open to solutions, i.e. different ways of doing things. Here, we go down a new path of inquiry, or create a different aspect to explore. Can we combine old ideas in new ways? Can we switch perspective? Here, we flex our more creative thinking skills—lateral, divergent, or systems thinking allows us to reach out and try something different:

What if we did nothing and let the sales team sort it out on their own?

What if the sales team worked from home from now on?

What if all this friction is a good thing?

What if the friction is alerting us to a bigger problem in the business?

As with all creative thinking, this step needs to be done without self-censorship or the fear of not finding a solution quickly enough. On the other hand, dwelling too long on the What if can result in stagnant "analysis paralysis"—that's where determining relevance will come in handy! You could follow each of the above questions with a more practical, concrete *How?* This will allow you to quickly disqualify ideas that won't practically work, and focus in on those with more real-world potential.

What if we do nothing? How? That's easy, we don't do anything, and check in a month to see the result.

What if they worked from home? How? That will be difficult. Some of the work needs to be done in person.

What if the friction is a good thing? How? On second thought, it does appear to have few advantages for anyone.

What if the friction is alerting us to a bigger business problem? How? We could start by asking the sales team what the problem is. How? We could conduct individual interviews and see if we can find a common answer, then decide if there's a bigger issue . . . and so on.

You'll notice that this kind of thinking is more or less an expanded version of the scientific method's: "If I do this, what will happen?" By combining both creative and analytical thinking skills, the problem is expanded and analyzed, allowing a methodical process that leads to a well-considered solution. We first stock our toolkit with as many useful tools as possible, and then devise a structured method for taking out each one in turn, when it's most needed and appropriate. This approach even allows us to devise new tools as necessary!

Another way to synthesize all these different aspects of thinking is called *reverse engineering*. The trouble with using different cognitive tools is that one size most certainly does not fit all. Sometimes, you need a tool that is so specific, it can literally only solve the very unique problem you have in front of you. In this case, reverse engineering can help you design that tool working from the solution backward, rather than trying to trial-and-error the tools you already have and hoping one fits.

The term is, obviously, borrowed from the engineering world, and refers to starting with a finished gadget or appliance, then deconstructing it to find out how it works, pulling apart its components to better understand how they function. This is in contrast to building the appliance from the ground up.

Any time we look at a finished problem or situation, we can reverse engineer it and ask, what happened to bring about this state of affairs? What circumstances and actors came together, and in what way, to produce this finished "product" (i.e. the problem or solution in front of you). We can also use this way of thinking to design a way of thinking itself, i.e. a mental tool. We can ask ourselves, what would it look like if I knew the answer here? What form would my solution take? What would be different if I didn't have this problem? In this way, you are starting from a finished tool (i.e. the solution) and working your way backward.

This can be tricky to do and takes time, but is enormously powerful when done properly. It's a line of questioning that allows for the generation of new ideas and for creative thinking, but all within a clearly delineated field of relevance—because you've already identified the end point or goal. Try out your proposed solutions/tools and see what happens.

If they worked, what worked and why? If not, what does it tell you about your tool? About the assumptions you used to make your tool? The process is iterative and dynamic. You can keep going as long as you're curious and want to improve on your process.

In the sales team example, we can consider the situation as it is as a complex social machine. How could we take it apart and look at how it works? If we wanted to design a machine that would result in *maximum* conflict and inefficiency, how would we do it, and what does it tell us about the *right* way to do things?

Whichever way we choose to use the many different cognitive tools at our disposal, there's no escaping the fact that problem solving, creativity, and analytical thought are best experienced and practiced, and not merely talked about. In that spirit, we'll turn our attention now to the more practical part of our book—the riddles themselves.

As you read through each one, try to resist the urge to leap ahead and read the answer without trying first! The real value of a riddle is in its *unsolved form*—see the answer too soon and you rob yourself of the chance to puzzle through it yourself. Read through the riddle, pause, and consider which of the thinking modes already discussed could come in handy. Slow down and become deliberate and obvious in your thinking. Ask yourself, what assumptions am I making? What kind of problem or question is this? What conventions am I relying on? Does this puzzle look like anything I've done before? And so on.

Lastly, don't get too frustrated if you simply can't figure a puzzle out. Some people relish a real challenge, but others will find themselves frustrated, at a dead end without any further insight. Remember, the goal of a riddle is not to find the answer, but to explore and strengthen the processes that allow you to find the answer.

These are only silly cognitive games—the real gain is to be had in the more finely developed sense of creative, analytical, and abstract thought you'll earn as a result of going through them. So, don't worry if a good few of these riddles completely stump you.

Takeaways:

- Riddles are phrases or questions framed in the form of puzzles that require all types of thinking to deduce its answer or some double meaning underlying its words. They employ several different patterns of thinking, challenging us to work with limited information in unique ways. No one style of thinking is better than the other. Each is useful in different situations, and we must grasp how to apply them correctly. This is exactly what riddles help us learn, since it involves many different thinking styles.

- The most important tool that helps solve riddles is divergent thinking. This form of thinking demands that you survey and analyze all possible solutions to any given problem. In its opposite, convergent (or critical) thinking, we generally operate within a set of rules and use them to work our way to arrive at answers. However, in divergent thinking, the rules are immaterial, and we must explore any and all relevant solutions.

- Other important tools include lateral thinking, which involves studying how we infer something from information given to us. Systems thinking calls on you to look at the bigger picture, namely how components of any idea or solution fit with one another to form a coherent whole. Lastly, inspirational thinking requires you to gain insight from some source, like a peak experience or an altered state of consciousness. This type of thinking lets our unconscious mind solve problems for us, allowing our conscious selves to benefit from it.

- A complete problem-solving strategy involves a certain sequence that combines all of these thinking frameworks. Often, the first step is to identify the specifics of the problem you're faced with. Following that, you need to evaluate the quality of the information available through research. Identify any biases you may have, and debate with yourself to recognize any holes in your logic.

Chapter 2. Situational Riddles

We'll start with a group of five riddles that have something in common: they are "situational" in nature. The puzzle lies in setting up a particular situation and asking what came before or what will come next. The situation is usually a little bizarre or inexplicable—with your task being to account for or explain the situation.

These riddles are like a little glitch in our ordinary understanding of the world. To solve them, the listener typically has to question or unpick their own biases or conventions. As you read, try to look well beyond the obvious details and content of the riddle and into its underlying structure. *Look at yourself thinking* and ask what you're doing to best solve the riddle. Once you've solved it, ask again why you were stumped in the first place, and what exactly allowed you to make the insight you did. Easier said than done!

The Man in the Bar

"A man walks into a bar and asks the bartender for a glass of water. The bartender then begins to search for something underneath the bar. Suddenly, he brings out a firearm and points it straight at the man. The man simply says, 'Thank you,' and immediately leaves."

The question for the reader is, *what happened?*

Let's attempt to completely clear our minds and look as closely as possible at this situation. By engaging in divergent ("opening up") thinking, we can start to expand our ideas not only of what potentially happens in bars, but about glasses of water, and guns. We can then use induction and inference to tentatively make guesses about information we don't yet have. There is clearly more to this story that we don't yet see! But what could it be?

Let's ask some questions to guide our thinking (many of which can be seen as clues):

Why did the man ask for a glass of water at a bar (and not, say, some kind of alcohol)?

Why did the man *not* give him what he wanted and instead threatened him with a gun?

Finally, why did the man say *thank you* instead of protesting being threatened?

These questions lead us down the right path. The gun must have, in some way, been something the man wanted. So, what is the connection between a glass of water and a gun? Use creative thinking to imagine the state of mind that would have you ask for a glass of water—and also what set of conditions would have you saying thank you to having a gun pointed in your face. How would you feel if someone pointed a gun at you—and why would you *thank* someone for making you feel this way?

What at first seems like a strange situation is actually rich with clues. In asking the above questions, you slowly start to question your assumptions about certain situations. We all have fixed ideas of what guns and glasses of water mean. But what else can they mean?

If you're ready to find out the answer, it follows: the man walking into the bar had hiccups, so he asked for a glass of water. Instead of giving him one, the bartender decided to scare away his hiccups with a gun instead. This worked, and the man leaves the bar, no longer needing his glass of water, and thanking the bartender for his help!

If you guessed the answer correctly, can you go back and see which questions helped you find it? Perhaps the insight came with imagining other creative and unconventional uses for water (not for thirst but to cure hiccups) and guns (not to threaten people but help them) or even fear (a good thing if it cures hiccups!). If you didn't get the riddle, *ask what exactly stopped you from seeing the "trick."*

Were you misdirected, or did you get stuck on only one possible explanation—for example, that having a gun drawn on you is always a bad thing? How could you avoid this trap in the future? You might decide to make a conscious effort to *not assume* what certain words, tools, ideas, or phrases mean. That in fact, much of their meaning derives from their context, and in solving problems of this nature, we have to carefully consider *why* a thing happens.

What starts out looking like a silly "gotcha!" riddle actually contains plenty of depth—it is only our fixed conceptual assumptions that limit us from seeing the potential in strange and unexpected situations. Remember that next time you are staring at a problem that seems completely incomprehensible!

Death in a Field

Feeling a little more warmed up? Let's try another situational riddle. As you read it, try to remember what you learned from the last riddle, and approach this one with as open a mind as you can manage.

"A man is lying in an open field, dead. Next to him lies an unopened package. There isn't another animal or person around him."

The question is, *how did the man die?*

Again, we are faced with a strange situation, in this case, the end result of a process we can't quite comprehend. Remembering what we learned from the previous example, we can perhaps start by assuming that things are not quite as they seem. Again, let's try to ask "a more beautiful question" and see where our analytical thinking takes us.

There isn't much information in the riddle, but we can start with the facts we *are* given. The riddle tells us no animal or other person is around, only an unopened package. It would seem that the package is connected to the man's death, and not some other agent, like a human or animal killer.

What do we know about packages *and* winding up dead?

Can we think of ways of dying that can happen in an open field (maybe you think of a heart attack, stroke, or simply death from old age)?

How many different kinds of packages can we think of (using divergent, creative thinking)?

What kinds of packages can result in a man's death, or at least accompany it? (You might think of a packet of poison, but then—this one was unopened. The question is, then, what kind of package kills by *not* being open? You may lead yourself down the path of imagining the man was already sick and desperately needed to open a package that contained the cure, but was too late. But then, what kind of condition could he have that happens without any other people or animals present? Could the package contain insulin?).

What information are we really missing here?

More importantly, can we use what we understand about riddles in general to help us find the answer? So many riddles create a diversion, throw out a "red herring," or deliberately obfuscate things. In what ways could this riddle be doing the same? In what ways are things being made to look more bizarre and unusual than they really are?

You might find yourself in the mindset of a detective who has to conduct very similar analyses of crime scenes, trying to piece together past events going only on clues left in the present.

If you'd like a clue, know that the man knew he was going to die just before he did.

If you're ready for the answer, it follows: the man jumped from an airplane but hit the earth when his parachute didn't open. It's his parachute that is the unopened package next to him.

What can we learn from this little puzzle? As with the previous example, things are not what they seem. We solve this riddle by expanding our understanding of what a "package" could be, and thinking outside the box. In this case, there weren't any animals or people around the man—but there was something in the sky. We might have heard "open field" and simply assumed this meant "the man is completely alone with nothing around him," causing us to completely overlook the extra dimension of the sky above.

This is a tricky puzzle that's possible to solve on your own—so long as you're able to connect the unopened package with a death, and avoid the diversion of thinking the man died of an illness. How many different kinds of packages did you imagine, and can you see now that your imagination could have taken you even further?

An Unusual Birth

By now, you must be getting familiar with the situational riddle format. That's good. You are developing new cognitive tools and becoming conscious of a great problem-solving truth: that the solution always lies well outside the conceptual bounds of the problem you find yourself in! Isn't it a marvelous muscle to strengthen—the ability to think of what you're not thinking of? Here's the next riddle.

"A woman gives birth to two sons; they are both born in the same hour, in the same day, in the same year. However, they are *not* twins."

The question is, *how could this be*?

This can be a very frustrating puzzle to work through. On the face of it, it is simply impossible that a woman can give birth to two sons at the same time without them being twins. Right? We know by now to abandon any fanciful ideas of how this might work biologically. More likely, the solution lies in the way we are conceptualizing childbirth, twins, etc., and the way we are using language.

Let's look at our assumptions that make us arrive at the conclusion that "this situation is not possible." The riddle tells us it *is* possible, so we need to dismantle these assumptions if we're going to find out exactly how.

Assumption: Humans take nine months to gestate, and a woman cannot give birth to another completely separate baby in the same hour after she's already given birth to one.

Assumption: The only way to have two babies at a time is to have them in twin form.

Focus on the truth of this second assumption, and you will find the solution—an annoyingly simple solution! Is it *really* true that the only way to have two babies at one time is through twins? We need to return to the facts: the woman gave birth to the two boys at the same hour, same day, same year. Respecting the ordinary limits of human reproduction, we are forced to imagine that nothing mystical has happened, and it's an ordinary birth. But then, our second assumption must be false somehow (here, we are using our analytical thinking and examining the logic in a deductive argument).

A hint comes in thinking along these lines: What are some ways of children being born that aren't twins and yet result in two babies being born? This is a way of formalizing the problem.

If you're ready for the answer, it's this: the two boys are not twins, but *triplets*.

Annoying, isn't it? If you failed to get this one, it should be easy to see why: you completely forget that more than one child can be born at one go, and when they are, they are called twins, triplets, etc. Like the sky in the previous riddle, we completely forget other potential dimensions to the situation. We back ourselves into a corner and assume that there are only two options: twins or single births.

Falling into this "either or" trap is a classic riddle trick. In real life, many problems are solved when we drop this kind of thinking and instead indulge in "this *and* that" thinking. By properly identifying the full field of possibilities, we see where our solution lies, and don't get distracted chewing over an artificially narrowed set of facts.

Adam and Eve

Let's take a look at our fourth situational riddle:

"A man dies and goes to heaven one day. There he discovers thousands of people, and all of them are naked. He scans around to try to find someone he might know. He then sees a couple and instantly recognizes them—they are Adam and Eve."

The question is, *how does the man know that they are Adam and Eve?*

This riddle is a little different from the others somehow. It seems very simple on the surface, and at first, the question doesn't seem all that challenging. But then, you realize that it would be difficult to recognize the literal Adam and Eve in the flesh, having never met them in person (assuming for a second here that you believe the Adam and Eve story is something that literally happened).

It would seem that the man immediately notices something about the man and woman that helps him confirm their identity. What could this distinguishing mark be? What do Adam and Eve possess that other humans don't? A big clue is in the fact that the riddle goes out of its way to explain that everyone is naked. This alerts us to the probability that the distinguishing feature is something that is seen when a person is naked, and might otherwise be hidden by clothing. (It also tells us that the distinguishing feature is not clothing itself—or something like a fig leaf!)

So, what do we know about Adam and Eve? Specifically, what do we know about the ways they might be different from others? After we've analyzed this line of thinking, can we imagine the ways that they're different that might be immediately visible if they were naked?

You might be seeing the answer by now. Adam and Eve are ordinary humans who don't in fact have differing features from average people—except for one thing. The key thing about Adam and Eve is that they're the *first* people.

The answer to the riddle is obvious: the man recognizes Adam and Eve because they are the only people who do not have belly buttons. Belly buttons or navels are a sign that you were once attached to your mother as you grew in her womb. Adam and Eve, being created directly by God, won't have them.

Granted, this riddle makes plenty of assumptions itself, and to solve it, you need to immerse yourself in the special mix of language, symbolism, and imagery that it exists within. This riddle requires a deeper knowledge of the story, but also a curiously practical, physiological take on it—so even those familiar with the story will have to practice a little lateral thinking. After all, every artistic depiction of Adam and Eve actually does show them with navels!

A Woman Shoots her Husband . . .

Let's consider one more situational riddle to practice. By now, you may be getting a good idea of the format of these riddles—as well as the cognitive blind spots and assumptions that stump you, if you haven't managed to solve some of them. Here's the riddle:

"A woman shoots her husband, then holds him underwater for five full minutes. A little later on in the day, they both go out for dinner and have a nice time together."

The question is, *how can this be? What happened?*

In the first riddle, with the man who asked the barman for a glass of water, the trick lies in the fact that ordinary objects and actions are used in unexpected ways. Because we can't imagine these ways, the situation looks strange to us. The moment we open our mind to other possibilities, however, the solution becomes obvious.

A similar thing is happening in this riddle. Let's consider the premise that we are faced with and dig a little deeper.

Assumption: shooting her husband and holding him underwater should kill him.

We already know it doesn't. This immediately tells us to reexamine our understanding of this shooting and this holding underwater. What else could they mean if not that she took a gun and literally murdered him, then held him underwater?

We can imagine all sorts of non-lethal ways to shoot someone and then hold them underwater. The gun may have been a water pistol and the husband may have been wearing a snorkel, and the woman then merely hugs (i.e. "holds") him underwater at the same time. In a sense, this is the "right" answer because it does adequately explain the situation. But then again, we could also propose other outlandish "solutions" like her husband is actually an amphibious and bullet-proof superhero and they always have fun on weekends by pretending to murder one another. These solutions are good because they show that a degree of creative thinking is taking place. But they are also unsatisfying in a way—perhaps because we feel that they haven't really solved anything, and that that insightful *aha* moment, that jump from conundrum to solution, never really happens.

The lateral thinking in this puzzle may be very obvious to some and frustrating to others. If you'd like a clue, it comes down to *words* being used in unexpected ways.

The solution is this: the woman is a photographer, and when she "shoots" her husband, it's with a camera. When she "holds him underwater for five minutes," it's really his photo that she is holding under developing solution in a dark room.

The solution emerges easily if we avoid leaping to assumptions (i.e. she shot him *with a gun*) and consider all possible meanings of the word "shoot" and the phrase "hold someone underwater." The creative skill comes in seeing that shooting and holding underwater belong to a completely different conceptual framework.

The trick is not to assume that your kneejerk assumption—that she killed with a gun—is true. Reading the riddle again, you see no mention of a gun. In real life, don't we all regularly assume what people mean when they use certain words or phrases? Couldn't we solve so many problems or have so many insights if we were simply to become aware that our language was arbitrary, ambiguous—or even that we were using language in the first place?

Takeaways:

- Situational riddles are those that involve some bizarre circumstances that have taken place. Your job is to account for or explain why the situation materialized in that particular way by challenging assumptions one commonly holds. The lowest hanging fruit in terms of solutions or reasoning almost never applies, so it's up to you to deduce what's really going on.
- Imagine a man who walks into a bar and asks the bartender for a glass of water. The bartender instead brings out a firearm and points it at the

man, who then promptly thanks him and leaves immediately. What happened here?

- Think about why the man asked for water, why he was offered a gunshot instead, and why he would thank the bartender for it. What use could water and a gun have in common? The answer is to get rid of hiccups. The fear of a gunshot chased the man's hiccups away just like a glass of water would.

- A man in an open field lies dead with an unopened package next to him. No animal or human is around him. How did he die?

- Think of the sorts of packages that can cause death without being opened. Using divergent thinking, we can deduce that one type of package is a parachute. The man had jumped out a plane and died because his parachute did not open.

- A woman gives birth to two sons born in the same hour of the same day. But they aren't twins. How? The key here is to think of how one can have two babies without being twins. There is a slight omission of information here. The simple answer is that they are triplets.

- Finally, a woman shoots her husband, then holds him underwater for five minutes. Later, they go out for dinner and have a nice time. What happened? Come up with non-lethal ways one can shoot someone and hold them underwater. Again, we have wordplay here. You'll eventually arrive at photography. The woman is a photographer shooting her husband with a camera. Holding him underwater is really his photo in developing solution.

Chapter 3. More Complex Analytical Riddles

As you've seen, the kind of riddle we explored in part one could be solved by switching perspective, questioning ordinary assumptions, and looking more closely at words, tools, or situations to find a hidden, overlooked aspect where the solution lies. These riddles are sometimes solved quickly in a flash of insight—you may or may not get them, but if you're stuck, it seldom makes it better to keep thinking.

Our next group of riddles, however, requires a little more than a quick shift in perspective or a flash of insight. Instead, these riddles are all about carefully picking your way through details to arrive at a logical conclusion.

The Riddle of Five Men

The riddle goes like this: "Five men are walking together. It starts to rain, and so four of the men speed up and walk more quickly; the fifth man doesn't try to pick up pace—yet he stays dry. The other four men, however, get wet despite trying to avoid it. The five men all arrive together at their destination at the same time."

Immediately, you can tell that this puzzle will require a different set of intellectual tools than our previous riddles. Let's put away the lateral and creative thinking and instead bring out the analytical thinking. Remember the important aspects of this way of thinking: first identification, then research, some inference, deduction or induction, determining relevance, and finally, curiosity.

Let's begin by identifying the problem. It seems on the surface impossible that four men should get wet while the other doesn't, despite them seemingly moving more or less together. The puzzle seems to be: what is different about the fifth man or what he is doing that results in him not getting wet when the others did?

There are many details to this puzzle, all of which need to be considered separately, then combined. The man makes no effort to stay dry and yet does. The men arrive together. A hint might help you narrow down the possible answers that might work here: not all of the men were on foot.

A possible scenario: the fifth man was in a car or other kind of vehicle, so he was shielded from the rain. However, this is a little weird—it would entail the men walking closely beside a slowly driving car. Bodyguards surrounding an important figure in a ceremonial car, for example? Another option is that the fifth man is ill somehow and lying down on a stretcher, being carried by the other four men. However, this would still result in the fifth man getting wet. Unless . . .

As you can see, another solution is possible. Here it is: The man is actually dead and being carried by the other four, who are the funeral's pallbearers. They run and get wet anyway, but the dead man doesn't because he is covered inside the coffin.

To arrive at this answer, you likely had to systematically work your way through possible solutions and decide whether they worked or not. Doing so brought you closer and closer to the answer, not so much by flash of insight but by methodical and logical steps. We can see this kind of thinking in real life all the time. Doctors do it when they perform differential diagnosis: "It can't be this, it can't be that, so that means it *must* be the third thing." You'll recognize this process as a form of deductive reasoning.

Riddles like this teach us to use conditionals in our thinking, or IF, THEN, AND, or BUT operators. We think along the lines of, "*If* the man was with the other four all along and didn't get wet, *then* he must have been covered somehow, or inside something else . . ." These are processes that we take for granted until a riddle like this shows us how important they are in problem solving!

The Murderer's Choice

Our second analytical riddle asks you to carefully consider a few options and then make your choice between them using whatever data you can. Here it is: "A murderer is found guilty and condemned to death in a rather cruel and unusual way. He is instructed to choose to open one of three possible doors. Behind the first is a room full of powerful raging fires; behind the second is a room full of deadly assassins with weapons, hellbent on killing him; in the third is a room with vicious lions who haven't eaten in years."

The question is, *which room would be the safest for the murderer to choose if he wanted the best chance of survival?*

Okay, thinking caps on. We'll need to use our analytical minds to unpick the relative risks associated with each choice. This parallels a lot of critical thinking tasks we all have to do in real life—choosing between different careers, different houses or areas to live in, even different romantic partners. How are we even going to start weighing up the risks of each room?

To start with, the raging fires seem pretty grim—would it really be possible to survive being burned alive? The second room doesn't look good either—one highly trained assassin could probably finish you off, not to mention a whole room full of them. Similarly, a room full of hungry lions could quickly make a meal of the man. Which would be the best choice?

If you're eagle-eyed or familiar with riddles, you may have easily spied the answer already. The truth is that the riddle only *seems* like a complex analytical puzzle on the surface—in reality, it's very, very simple. It's as though we are primed to see three choices and then immediately begin weighing them up (not to mention this book is deliberately misleading you as well . . . sorry about that!). Have you spotted the obvious clue that makes all this analysis unnecessary?

The answer to the riddle follows: the third room is the safest, because all the lions would be dead, since they "haven't eaten in years." If you're groaning and rolling your eyes now, it's probably because you were caught out by what you *thought* the riddle was asking, rather than looking very clearly at what it was actually saying.

There is a similar riddle that asks a person a series of complex mathematical questions to do with age, and finishes with the question, so how old are you? The answer is to simply say how old you are—the rest of the riddle was nothing more than an elaborate red herring.

It's worth looking closely at admittedly annoying riddles such as this one. Sometimes ordinary life really does appear to us as more complex than it really is. Being used to solving things in a particular way, we race ahead and solve it using the method we think we're being asked to use, completely missing the obvious and simple answer staring us in the face.

The person thinks he is facing a multiple-choice question where he is meant to sum up the relative risks (and to be fair, the riddle sets him up in this way). In other words, people only *think* they know what is being presented: three very dangerous rooms. What this riddle also does is play with conceptual frames. The person hearing it might assume that "haven't eaten in years" is simply a figure of speech or an exaggeration for effect. Tackling riddles like this teaches us something both profound and simple: read the instructions thoroughly!

A Poison Riddle

Let's try another analytical riddle and flex our skills a little more:

"Two girls are at a restaurant eating dinner together. They both order the iced tea to drink. The first girl drinks hers very quickly and orders and drinks four more iced teas, all in the time it takes the second girl to slowly drink just one glass. It turns out, the drinks were actually poisoned. However, the girl who drank five iced teas in total was not killed, whereas the girl who drank just one died."

The question is, *how did the girl survive? And why did the other one die?*

Let's start at the beginning. There is a lot of information in this riddle that immediately stands out as odd. We can see that, strangely, the girl who drank more of the iced tea didn't die, while the girl who drank less did. This is completely opposite to what we'd expect. We have to then assume that the poison is not what we're imagining—what kind of poison behaves in this strange way?

We would expect a poison to be more deadly the more it was consumed. Let's follow this line of thinking further—is there a way for someone to drink a lot of poison and actually fare better because of it? We might imagine that the girl who drank five teas actually threw up from it and was thus saved, but the other girl slowly drank a little, didn't throw up, and was killed. This is possible, but not the right answer yet. We have to keep playing detective.

Maybe you're getting the idea that the *tea* and the *poison* could be separate things. This is a clue. Earlier in this book, we discussed systems thinking and the ability to see how all the parts of a whole connect and influence one another. This allows us to think of aspects of the problem we've overlooked, and see their influence on the situation. Here's a clue: iced tea contains *two* main ingredients, one of which changes with time.

The solution is this: the poison in the iced tea was actually *in the ice* and not the tea. The first girl drank five glasses so quickly, the ice never had time to melt and poison her, whereas the other waited until the ice melted, then drank the poison and died. By simply hearing "iced tea" and imagining some homogenous beverage, we instantly miss the solution to the riddle.

Scientific researchers actually face this problem in real life all the time. "Hidden variables" can completely ruin studies because they make it hard to tease out cause and effect relationships. For example, someone might claim that there's a link between drinking wheatgrass juice and longevity, assuming that one caused the other, but it's actually a *third*, hidden variable that is causing both the presence of wheatgrass juice and increased longevity: being wealthy.

Similarly, we assume that it's the iced tea in its entirety that is responsible for causing death, when it's actually only one aspect of it—the ice. When trying to understand why something happens, it's crucial to tease out the separate variables so that we don't make the kind of mistake we might make trying to solve this riddle, i.e. assuming that iced tea is simpler than it really is!

The Window Cleaner

Let's try another one. This riddle, like most riddles, will challenge you to think out of the box—or show you all the ways that you were stuck in the box in the first place!

"A window cleaner is busy cleaning windows on the twenty-fifth floor of a skyscraper. He suddenly slips and falls, and yet he isn't harmed, despite not wearing any safety equipment or a harness."

The question is, *how could this be? How could he survive the fall?*

Quite the puzzle, isn't it? Have you started to dream up all the various things the window cleaner could have fallen onto to save his life? Congratulations—your brain is practicing creative, divergent thinking. Maybe he fell into a pool of water, a trampoline, or similar, and was unharmed. But I'm sure you can guess that the answer is not that simple (in fact, it's simpler!).

Like many riddles, you may end up spending a lot of time thinking of solutions in entirely the wrong direction. We start out with an unquestioned assumption or bias and run with it, never noticing that we did so, and unable to change track once we start down one line of thinking. This is why it's so important to open the mind and really look at what's in front of you. No riddle was ever solved by brute force. And no mind-bending problems were solved by merely digging deeper and deeper into the same old rut that doesn't ever get you anywhere.

So, rather than trying to imagine exactly *how* the man can fall off a skyscraper and not die, simply imagine that . . . he doesn't.

Have you discovered the answer yet? The fact is, falling off a skyscraper from twenty-five stories would kill anyone. The man doesn't die, so therefore, he must *not* have fallen from twenty-five stories. This little bit of deductive reasoning seems too simple, but it's the key to solving the puzzle.

The answer is this: the window cleaner was cleaning windows from *inside* the building.

The brain is a wonderful thing, and it works hard for us all the time, constantly taking mental shortcuts and using fixed concepts, assumptions, and biases to quickly work out the world around us. Our brains make best guesses, fill in the gaps, and infer what a thing should be, using very little contextual information most of the time. Do you see how quickly and easily you assumed that the window cleaner was on the outside? You made this assumption so quickly, it seemed all but invisible to you. You believed you were dealing with the plain facts of the riddle, but your brain had already leapt ahead to fill in some details where they didn't strictly exist.

Creative thinkers and expert problem-solvers don't do this. They get into the habit of constantly asking what they take for granted, what they assume, what guesses they've made, and they never allow themselves to assume these guesses are facts. Someone might get tangled up in trying to solve a problem that they don't realize *they've* introduced merely in the way they've formulated things. The doctor could feel stumped after desperately trying to decide which disease his patient has. But in all this, he never considers one possibility: his patient *isn't* sick. He doesn't see this possibility because his first (hidden) assumption was that there was a disease, and his job was to find it out.

The next time you're solving a really complex or tricky problem, take the time to literally write down all your assumptions— even and especially the very obvious ones. Then question each one. You may find your solution hidden right there, not in the problem itself, but in your automatic conception of it.

Say My Name

Our final riddle has a somewhat old-school feeling to it—it's short and deceptively simple.

It goes like this: "What disappears the moment you say its name?"

Your brain may immediately start thinking of things that might run away when named, until you realize that, since this is a riddle, the answer is not likely to be the most obvious, ordinary thing. This can be a really easy riddle, or it can totally stump you— just like some people can instantly see the hidden figure in a "magic eye" puzzle while others never do.

Let's start, as usual, by becoming curious and asking some questions, or imagining some scenarios.

Can you think of some thing or animal that runs away when you say its name?

Could it be that it's not a thing or animal so much as an idea or concept?

What idea disappears when spoken out loud?

Or, what thing is very different from a spoken aloud name?

Perhaps this last question has already given you a big clue to what the answer is. The riddle is telling us that something disappears when you speak out loud—what stops, ends, or disappears when we speak out loud? Well, what's the opposite of speaking out loud?

The answer is this: *silence.*

As you can see, this is yet another riddle that asks us to step outside our ordinary ideas, assumptions, and concepts, and find the solution in a place we wouldn't think to look at first. The first hurdle is to understand that this "it" is not a physical thing—in fact, the entire puzzle can be solved when we think of silence (ordinarily an absence of a thing rather than a thing itself) as a thing with a name.

This elegantly shows us the built-in assumptions (and limits) of our language, and somehow has a poetic quality too. With a creative and open mindset, we can start to imagine a far wider range of "things" than the ordinary world typically expects from us. We are invited to step outside of the normal world of named objects and think a level higher up—to a conceptual plane where the *absence of a thing* can also have a name, and furthermore, we are invited to come down out of that conceptual level afterward to understand that *speaking* the name immediately destroys silence. What a lot to contain in just one small question.

Takeaways:

- Analytical riddles are more challenging than situational ones because instead of shifting perspectives, they require you to carefully analyze information to arrive at conclusions. This is the classic comparison of divergent versus convergent thinking. It might be easier depending on your proclivities, but often, the devil is in the details.

- Five men are walking together when it starts to rain. Four of them start walking quickly, while the fifth doesn't. Yet he stays dry, and the other four get wet. They all arrive at their destination at the same time. How?
- Logically examining the details reveals the answer, the fifth man was dead and being carried in a coffin by the other four. This is how he did not get wet, didn't pick up pace, and yet reached his destination at the same time as the others. This was some kind of funeral situation.
- A window cleaner is cleaning windows on the twenty-fifth floor of a skyscraper when he slips and falls, yet isn't harmed despite not wearing any safety equipment. How?
- It is easy to fall into the trap of thinking of ways one can fall twenty-five floors without dying, but the answer here is that he never does. He was cleaning the windows from inside the building.

- Two girls order iced teas at a restaurant. The first girl drinks hers quickly and orders four more, while the other drinks her first one slowly. The teas were poisoned, but only the second girl dies. How?
- Think of the ingredients in iced tea: ice and tea. This reveals the solution, wherein the ice was poisoned. Thus, the second girl dies because her ice has more time to melt, whereas the first girl escapes this by drinking her tea quickly.

- Finally, what disappears the moment you say its name? Think of what the opposite is to saying something aloud. It's silence, which is what disappears when you say something.

Chapter 4. Brain Teasers

The next group of riddles is concerned again with analytical thinking, and the work your brain has to do to unravel and tease out a solution from a string of complicated facts. The puzzles that follow rely less on flashes of insight or conceptual leaps, and more on raw processing power. In solving them, you will become immediately aware of all the little cognitive shortcuts and assumptions your brain makes—and how these can actually stand in the way of you solving a problem quickly and efficiently.

Like the "Say My Name" riddle, we are asked to look at the problem in a novel way, but in these riddles, there are a host of things we are invited to turn on their heads and look at more closely: words and their meanings, the way we use tools, and our ordinary understanding of cause and effect.

Again, as you read through each one, try to give yourself enough time to answer it before checking the answer. You may surprise yourself and solve it all at once after ruminating over a seemingly impossible puzzle for ages.

The Dark Cabin

Let's begin with a riddle that teaches us to approach every new problem or puzzle with a completely fresh mind. Can we look at the "riddles" in our own life without any preconceived ideas, prejudices, or expectations at all? It's harder to do than you think!

Sometimes, when we face a challenge or a problem that requires our action, we automatically *assume what kind of problem it is*, and it's this assumption that narrows down the potential solutions we're willing to consider. The whole point of a problem is that we're unfamiliar with what we're seeing—those who can truly appraise a puzzle with "fresh eyes" and no beliefs about the form the answer should take are far more likely to see the way out.

Think about this as you attempt the following riddle:

"You are in a dark cabin, and all you have is a single match in a matchbox, a candle, some newspaper, and an oil stove. The question is, which do you light first?"

Without you knowing it or having much control over it, your brain has likely already shot off to try to solve the problem in the way it thinks it should be solved. Maybe you're thinking along the lines of, "Well, if I've only got one match, then I had better spend it wisely. Which thing will be easiest to light? I could light that thing first and then use it to light the other things to bring light to the cabin . . ." and so on.

Why does your brain think this? Because it *thinks* it's solving the problem. Isn't this what the riddle is asking us, to figure out which is the best thing to light first so that we have the best chance of filling the cabin with light? But read the riddle again and see if this is what it's really asking, or if it's merely what we *think* it's asking.

This line of thinking quickly goes nowhere—you could conceivably light any of them. Would it really make a difference which one you chose first? But read the riddle again. Which one do you light first?

If you're ready for the answer, it's this: you light the match first!

This somewhat frustrating riddle shows us a few clever things. First, that people often rush ahead to solve a problem at a higher level than is strictly necessary. Many of the riddles we've heard require you to take a conceptual step up, as it were. This one, however, asks you to take a step *down* and simply solve the immediate, obvious question staring you in the face. In getting carried away with a higher order problem, we completely miss what the riddle has asked. It's the equivalent of not really reading the question in an exam, or assuming that your computer is broken in a complicated way when actually it's just not plugged into the wall.

This riddle shows us something else: often, we actually do find the answer and yet *don't know it*, making us carry on looking—which is essentially the same as not having the answer. Of course, we know that we have to light the match first. Sometimes, the hardest problems in life are "solved" by simply reframing them as not problems at all. Sometimes, you fret and ruminate over a potential solution and completely ignore the fact that you already know how to fix it, you only dismissed the solution long ago because it seemed too obvious and simple.

Finally, this riddle teaches us to check our assumptions. Occasionally, the biggest obstacle to our critical thinking is the fact that we are too attached to old ways of solving problems and habits we've learned from previous problems (we can blame school for teaching us the same tired old formats for problems). The next practical riddle you face, ask if it's actually a problem at all, and if it is, is the solution a ridiculously obvious one? Have you already solved it without acknowledging you did?

A Strange Word

Are you ready to try again with a related riddle? As you read through the next riddle, try to remember to see only what is strictly in front of you, and don't take any of your assumptions too seriously!

The riddle goes like this: "What five-letter word becomes shorter when you add two letters to it?"

Let's pause and take it slowly. What do we see in the riddle above? It looks at first to be a contradiction. Everything that we know about the way that words and spelling works is that if you add letters to a word, it becomes longer. In fact, adding anything to anything else and winding up with less is simply something that's not arithmetically sound or logical, no matter how you cut it.

So, what does this tell us? It's a clue that our assumptions above are not going to work for us with this riddle. There is something

90

about the idea "adding to a thing makes it longer, not shorter" that holds the key to solving this riddle.

Inspired by what we've learned from the previous riddles, let's try to examine our assumptions a little more closely. We are assuming this riddle wants us to think of a special word that magically becomes shorter when two letters are added. And yet we know this is logically impossible. What we need to do, perhaps, is abandon this line of thinking altogether, and ask: in what *other ways* can adding letters to a word make it shorter? We want to think not of a special word, but a special *way* in which to add letters to a word, i.e. there's no point trying to think of individual words—there are none.

Here's a clue: the riddle you just read above is itself made of words.

Have you spotted the trick yet?

If you need another clue: think about the two different ways in which a thing can "become shorter," bearing in mind that a word and the idea of a word are two different things.

The answer is simple: the word is *short*. When you add two letters to it, it becomes *shorter*.

If you solved the puzzle, well done! If not, can you think of why the answer eluded you?

The trick lies in understanding that the riddle is pointing directly to the word in the riddle itself. A similar riddle is, "What makes you young? The letters 'ng.'" What we see here is a game with referee and referent, with a thing and the symbol we put on a thing to help us understand it. As readers, we assume that the words in the riddle are pointing elsewhere, even forgetting that we are using words at all. We can only solve it by changing perspective and considering the very conceptual tools that the riddle employs.

A real-life equivalent is wondering for ages why everyone tested in a hospital has the same rare disease, before understanding the reason why: the test is faulty. We can all too easily forget that sometimes the problem we face is not actually embedded in reality itself, but in the signs, symbols, and conceptual tools we use to talk about that reality. In the same way that we can ask what assumptions we are using, we can also ask what tools we're using—remembering that words are the most ubiquitous and invisible tools of all.

A Strange Sum

Now that you've had a chance to puzzle through the previous riddle, the following one should be a little easier to solve. In the previous problem, it was words that stumped us; in this one, it's going to be numbers.

The riddle goes like this: "How can you add two to eleven and get one as the correct answer?"

What tools have we learned from previous riddles that could help us work through this one?

We could question our assumptions and look closely at the way we are assuming the puzzle ought to be solved. Or we could consider that what seems impossible at first is possible, so long as we completely shift our frame of understanding.

Just as it was in the puzzle above, it is arithmetically incorrect to say 11 + 2 = 1. However, the riddle tells us that one is in fact the correct answer. This tells us that these numbers are not in the ordinary realm of what we're thinking of. A sum like 11 + 2 is purely abstract—they're just numbers. But can we imagine a real-world example where the abstract laws of math don't hold in this way?

The "Strange Word" riddle taught us to look at *how* we're using symbols, so let's do that here: if we can't solve this riddle using ordinary numbers and ordinary arithmetic, what other ways can we use instead? Try to think of all the ways we use numbers in real life. Do any of them display this strange behavior?

If you still haven't gotten the answer, here it is: by adding two hours to 11 o'clock, you get 1 o'clock.

So, we have used numbers not as digits but almost as tags on a twelve-hour clock. Usually, thirteen follows twelve, but under special twelve-hour clock rules, it's perfectly correct to progress to one from twelve. It is true that one never follows twelve in an arithmetic sense, but the puzzle is asking us to imagine a different case entirely. We only need to understand that numbers can act in different ways, sometimes as digits, sometimes as ranks, and sometimes referring to ideas or quantities that have their own laws and rules.

Taking and Making

See if you can use your ability to shift perspectives in the following riddle. You'll recognize the ways it's similar to the previous riddles.

It goes like this: "What makes more as you take them?"

We already know that the answer to this riddle with resolve any apparent contradiction we see on first hearing it. We see these words that seem to disagree with one another: *make* and *take* seem to be opposites. Just as with the "shorter" riddle and the clock riddle above, we can see that to solve this, we will have to question and even undo our ordinary understanding of what it means to make and to take something.

Can we think of something that increases the more we take it?

As you can probably guess, the clue is in the word "take" and how we use it. Can you think of ways to take something that doesn't decrease, but increase?

Perhaps you've thought of photographs— the more you take, the more photographs there are (a gain). We also speak of "taking action" even though we use *take* here in a different sense, i.e. we mean undertake or do rather than take *away*.

The answer is this: footsteps. The more footsteps you take, the more footsteps there are.

For this riddle, however, you may have come up with plenty of other creative solutions that are not strictly incorrect. You might have imagined a water well—the more you take, the more water appears. You could have also gone a bit more abstract; for example, the more clutter you remove from a house, the more space you have inside. As we did in the "Say My Name" riddle, we simply need to reframe empty space as a thing in the same way as we do clutter.

This puzzle can be solved merely by understanding that some words can have multiple meanings. Even though we see a contradiction at first, it vanishes when we consider alternative meanings for the same word.

The Man, the Car, and the Hotel

We'll finish this section with a riddle in the same family. We've looked at how our assumptions about numbers, words, and concepts can trip us up and keep us from seeing the solution—we'll take this idea further in this riddle and look at how important *context* is.

The shortcuts our brain makes are usually to our benefit—right up until we are faced with a truly unique and novel situation. Then, our mental models fail us, and our cognitive shortcuts can actually lead us down the wrong paths. Some riddles seem to be designed to artificially violate our ordinary assumptions, but there are certainly instances in real life where there is a problem in one perspective, which disappears the moment you shift into a different perspective.

This kind of lateral, out-of-the-box problem solving is not routinely taught in schools, but is arguably more valuable than simply knowing how to solve rote problems from memory or an ingrained sense of convention. When was the last time you solved a truly novel problem, or sincerely looked at something in a completely new way? Though the following riddle is contrived and silly once you understand the "trick," it points to something bigger in the way we usually think: that we rely heavily on context and habit to tell us what something means.

The riddle goes like this: "A man takes his car to a big hotel, and the moment he arrives there, he is instantly declared bankrupt."

The question is, *why?*

We could imagine that the man was on the brink of bankruptcy, and the last straw was reached coincidentally as he arrived at the hotel. Perhaps something happened at the hotel to trigger his bankruptcy, like meeting with his accountant who officially declares it. Though this is all plausible, by this point in the book, you probably know that the answer will have to be a little more than this!

We could guess that there's something meaningful about the hotel, the car, and the man going bankrupt. What could their relationship be? Or more importantly, can we imagine a particular context where this scenario does not seem strange, but completely run of the mill?

Let's begin with questions.

What is the relationship between the man and the hotel? Does he own it maybe, or is he visiting? There to do business?

How could someone know that they have immediately become bankrupt simply by being in a place?

Can we imagine a totally different context to the ordinary—i.e. what other contexts include cars, hotels, and going bankrupt as the norm?

The answer to this riddle is this: the man is playing the game Monopoly, with the car piece as his token. When he lands on a square with a hotel belonging to another player, he realizes he'll have to pay more than he has, and declares bankruptcy.

Sometimes scientific researchers or anthropologists are puzzled by some new finding or bit of data—until they consider where it came from. When they put certain crucial details into place, it all makes sense. They realize their data is impossible when applied to creatures on earth, but not for deep sea animals, for example, or they understand that what is perceived as threatening in one culture is actually welcoming in another. The facts of the problem haven't changed—only the context has. We'll consider context in a later chapter.

Takeaways:

- The following set of riddles exploits the cognitive shortcuts and assumptions our brain makes.
- You are in a dark cabin and you have a single match in a matchbox, a candle, a newspaper, and an oil stove. Which do you light first?
- The answer is to light the match first. We generally disregard the match and focus on the other three options,

yet the match is the obvious and correct answer.

- What five-letter word becomes shorter when you add two letters to it? Seemingly contradictory, the answer is the word short, where adding e and r makes it "shorter." These types of riddles often include the solution within the question itself.

- How can you add two to eleven and get one as the correct answer? This riddle appears to be mathematically impossible, since 11+2 cannot equal 1. However, the context matters. Adding two hours to 11 o'clock yields 1 o'clock, which is the correct answer.

- What makes more as you take them? There can be multiple correct answers to this one, as long as the object fulfils the condition that it increases the more we take it. Photographs and footsteps are both examples of this.

- A man takes his car to a big hotel, and the moment he arrives there, he is instantly declared bankrupt. Why? Again, analyze the context. In what world does arriving at a hotel cause bankruptcy? The answer is Monopoly, where the car piece is the man's token, and arriving at a hotel results in bankruptcy.

Chapter 5. More Classic Brain Teasers

As you make your way through these riddles, you're likely learning new ways of seeing information, new mental tools, new ideas about how to approach the unknown. To simply think about the way you're thinking (metacognition) is already a giant leap. We'll soon look at many more riddles, but at the end of the book, we'll try to synthesize all the skills you may have gathered along the way. Riddles are fun, but they're even better when you imagine them as training for higher-stakes, real-world problems after you close the book.

What Am I?

Here's the next riddle: "I don't have a voice, but I speak to you. I tell you all the things that people in the world do. I have leaves but I'm not a tree; I have a spine but am not a human; I have hinges but am not a door. What am I?"

Even if you have never heard this particular riddle before, you may well recognize the tone and format ("I have this but am not a that . . ."). After the previous riddles, you may well have immediately spotted the way to solve this: the item has leaves, a spine, and hinges, only not in the ordinary way. It "speaks" but not in the usual way.

This tells us that the riddle relies on a simple word game. Can we think of other, unexpected meanings or uses for leaves, spines, and hinges? Can you think of one single item that has all three of these things, but not in the expected way? The answer might be obvious to bibliophiles: it's a *book*. You may have also guessed an encyclopedia. We solve the riddle by searching our mental databases for the one item that possesses all these characteristics, understanding that the concept is a little different from the more standard one.

A Dog Crosses a River

Let's dive right into the next one: "A man is on one side of a river, and his dog is on the other. The man calls his dog, and the dog immediately crosses the river, despite there being no bridge of any kind or a boat. The dog reaches the other side without getting wet."

The question is, *how did the dog do it?*

Again, on the surface, we have a seeming impossibility. What set of conditions can explain and justify these facts? The main problem seems to be our assumption: "Going into a river makes you wet." I'm sure you can see where I'm going with this: can you imagine a special kind of river that *doesn't* make you wet when you cross it? Or can you imagine a special way for a dog to cross a river that means it doesn't get wet?

Maybe you imagine the dog crossing the river in a giant waterproof hamster ball, or imagine that the river is really small and can simply be leapt across. These are all legitimate answers, since they draw on your creative thinking prowess. But barring the dog owning some kind of rocket pack or having Jesus-like abilities to walk on water, you might soon turn to the river as the source of the problem. But aren't all rivers wet? Remember, there is no bridge, not even a series of rocks to hop along, and even if the river was very shallow, the dog would still get his paws wet, which he does not. Yet, he crosses the river. Something must be wrong with our assumptions!

Is it *really* true that all rivers are wet?

For some people, that may be enough of a clue. When someone says "river," what pops into your mind? Is that really the only way for a river to be?

By now you might have guessed the answer: the river that the dog crossed is actually frozen.

Don't worry if you didn't get it. We all have mental models and fixed concepts we conjure when we hear certain words. But of course, real life is a lot more complex and varied than our necessarily simplified mental models—i.e. the map is not the territory. Any word, symbol, idea, or concept is necessarily made simpler than it really is. Though we understand that rivers can freeze and completely change their properties and characteristics, the truth is that our mental image of "river" is very basic and inaccurate, probably corresponding poorly to real-life rivers everywhere.

Also consider the element of time in your problem solving, and make room for the fact that some aspects will change or take on many different forms. This is an extra variable seldom considered. How did this enormous fish find its way into this tiny pond that's shut off from the larger river? There's no miracle—it simply swam into the pond when it was little. The next time you read a word on a page that is intended to point to a real-life phenomenon in the world, remember that it is just a word, and that the thing itself is often more varied, more complex, and more interesting than the symbols we use to talk about it!

A Man in the Rain

Let's continue with the theme of water and getting wet. The next riddle goes like this: "A man is out walking, and it begins to rain. He's in the middle of nowhere with nowhere to hide, no umbrella, no hat or hood, and nothing at all to cover himself with. In fact, when he arrived home, he was completely soaked through. However, not a single hair on his head was wet. Why?"

Okay, let's run through the more ordinary possibilities—maybe the rain stopped long enough for the man's super fine hair to dry? Maybe, but this doesn't explain why his clothes were soaked through; surely they would have dried a little as well if his hair had time to dry?

As we've learned to do, let's explore the full realm of possibilities by looking not so much at the problem itself, but *the method by which we're attempting to solve the problem*. The riddle goes to great lengths to explain that the man was not wearing a hat or any protection over his head, so we can eliminate this as a possibility. There is no point in trying to imagine how he covered his head—we will probably have to look down a different avenue.

Is there a way to walk that exposes your entire body to the rain, but not your head? Maybe you can imagine a freakish man who can somehow tuck his head under his shoulder like a bird. Still, once we are in the realm of bizarre solutions, we may be flexing our creativity, but it's not really a true solution yet.

Let's read the riddle again and be sure that we've understood what is being asked of us. The riddle says, "Not a single hair on his head was wet." Have you guessed it yet?

The answer is: the man was bald!

Paul the Butcher's Assistant

Have you begun to notice the recurrent theme in this group of riddles? Great—you are not only learning to solve individual puzzles, but learning to seek patterns across all the riddles you encounter, forming a bank of data internally that you can draw on every time you see a new riddle or puzzle. This is metacognition again.

Here's the next riddle: "Paul is an assistant at a butcher's shop. He is a little over six feet tall and wears a size nine shoe. What does Paul weigh?"

If you've internalized some of the riddle-busting techniques we've practiced in the rest of this book, you may have solved this puzzle pretty quickly—well done! If not, continue using some of the mental tools we've mentioned already. Read the riddle again. Ask what your assumptions are, and question whether they're correct. Are you making any unfounded guesses about what's being asked of you?

Look at the way that words, symbols, and contexts are being used, played with, or violated. Look at the way you're thinking and ask if you can do it completely differently! If you can't wait any longer to find the answer out, it's this: what does Paul weigh? Meat. Because he's a butcher's assistant!

If you were caught out, don't worry. Just notice why it happened. It was the way the riddle was put forward that set you up. In cognitive psychology, this effect is called "priming," i.e. you were encouraged down a particular cognitive path by first being shown certain details, but these were really red herrings or distractions. Your brain automatically looks for patterns and tries to make the things it sees into a coherent whole. This means you interpret "weigh" in light of the other details, like height and shoe size. But look at how different this riddle is:

"Paul is an assistant at a butcher's shop, and is learning to be a butcher. Using the big scales near the checkout, what does he weigh?"

In fact, it's no longer a riddle at all. This can teach us a few important things about our expectations. When we have a fixed idea of what things are, we can sometimes fail to see a solution staring us right in the face. It's important, when solving problems, to not allow prior expectation, preconceived bias, or anything else cloud what you're really looking at. With a clear mind, you can see the problem for what it is—and solve it faster.

What Is It?

Our last riddle in this section relies on all the same tricks we are by now well familiar with. We are confronted with a seeming contradiction and asked to explain it; by using our regular ideas and beliefs, we don't understand, but by expanding our mind, we see a new scenario, meaning, or idea, and the problem is solved.

It goes like this: "The person who makes it has no need for it. The person who buys it isn't the one who uses it. The person who uses it doesn't even know they are using it. So, what is it?"

There are a few things that fit this bill—for example, a baby crib. The woodworker who builds it may not have children themselves, the person buying it is the parent who won't use it directly, and the baby who does use it is completely unaware they do. This is a great answer! Can you think of any more items like this? Hint: try to think of the kind of person who may be utterly unaware of themselves using something.

You may have thought of someone in a mental institution who takes medicine bought for them by doctors, made by manufacturers who will never take it themselves. The "official" answer to this problem is: a coffin. But that doesn't mean your solutions are wrong if they satisfy the criteria!

This riddle is an easy teaser that gently turns around our usual assumptions about buying things, i.e. that the person buying something is the one who uses it, and always knows they are. This riddle may be more fun, in fact, the more things you can come up with other than a coffin that fit the description. Perhaps a certain kind of poison intended to kill someone? Or an engagement ring before it's given?

Takeaways:

- This chapter contains more riddles that challenge normal ways of thinking.
- I don't have a voice, but I speak to you. I tell you all the things that people in the world do. I have leaves, but I'm not a tree; I have a spine but am not human. I have hinges but am not a door. What am I?
- Think of something that has leaves, spines, and hinges. Bibliophiles will recognize that the answer is a book. Through its words, it "speaks" without having a voice, its pages are leaves, and the binding forms its spine and hinges.
- Next, a man and his dog are on opposite sides of a river. The man calls his dog, who immediately crosses the river without a bridge, boat, or any other assistance. He also crosses over without getting wet. How? Focus on the river. What type of river can be crossed without getting wet, or without a bridge or boat? The answer is a frozen one.

- A man is out walking when it begins to rain. He's in the middle of nowhere, with nowhere to hide and nothing to cover himself with. He arrives home completely soaked, but not a single hair on his head is wet. How? Is there a way a man can be soaked without a single hair on his head being wet? This can only be possible if the man is bald, which is the right answer.

- Paul is an assistant at a butcher's shop. He is a little over six feet tall and wears a size nine shoe. What does Paul weigh? The last line might trick you into trying to deduce Paul's weight, but the answer is he weighs meat, because he is a butcher's assistant!

- The person who makes it has no need for it. The person who buys it doesn't use it, and the person who uses it doesn't know why they are using it. What is it? An obvious answer might be a baby crib, but the official one is a coffin.

Chapter 6. Context Riddles

Our final section will take a look at those brain teasers that rely heavily on us being able to "change the lens," cognitively speaking. In much the same way as we needed to understand that the bankrupted man was only playing a game of Monopoly, the following riddles can only be solved when we try to work backward from the problem—asking ourselves what set of circumstances would make the details we're hearing make sense.

This last batch may inadvertently strengthen your reverse engineering mental muscles, allowing you to assume that the facts you're given are correct and to try to work out exactly how they could be so. Like an engineer taking apart a lamp that works to see how it does, we can slowly work out what initially seems strange or mysterious to us.

Stolen Goods

Bearing the above in mind, let's jump into the next riddle. Remember to constantly check your assumptions, suspend any expectations, and simply look at the facts you're faced with. You might even find that the *less* you try to figure it out, the easier it is to do!

The riddle goes like this. "A woman goes into a big store and piles a shopping cart to the brim with things. Without paying for the items, she then leaves the store, and nobody attempts to stop her or call the police."

The question is, *how did the woman get away with it? What happened here?*

Let's gather up all the facts we can about this riddle. We are told the woman is in a store, that she fills her cart with things, leaves without paying, and nothing happens. Again, your mind may immediately start trying out certain outlandish solutions—maybe the woman was looting a mall during a zombie apocalypse and there simply was no surviving human around to see her. Maybe she had entered a strange game show where she was allowed to keep the items she could put into her cart in one minute. Or she had . . . an invisibility cloak?

By now, you know that these answers are a great sign of creative thinking and not "wrong" (remember, there are no wrong answers when we practice divergent, open-ended brainstorming!), but at the same time, there is something more here. We have to imagine what *perfectly ordinary* scenario might occur that would result in the facts we've just heard, without resorting to alien abductions, superpowers, or time travel.

Let's think slowly and carefully, unpicking each of our assumptions and premises like an engineer would take apart the workings of an appliance. The woman is *not* stopped or apprehended. What can we infer? That she is not in fact doing something illegal, and that her actions are not suspicious in the least.

How could that be? Let's follow this line of thinking. What kind of objects might you take without anyone expecting you to pay for them? What items have no dollar value or what items might people be glad you took, despite not paying for them?

Let's consider some other factors. What kind of a woman specifically may be able to take things in and out of a store without arousing suspicion (A nun? A famous politician who is preparing to do a photoshoot outside the store with a cart full of groceries?).

Finally, let's read the riddle again to make sure we're not inserting our own assumptions or missing a crucial detail just because we think we know what is being asked. Notice that the riddle doesn't say that the cart is filed with groceries, clothing, or indeed items from the store she is in.

Perhaps you are beginning to formulate your own possibilities.

If you're ready for the answer, it's this: the woman is an employee of the store (did you catch this?), and all she has piled into the cart is trash. When she takes this outside to throw in the dumpster, nobody bats an eyelid, since she's just doing her job.

Now, let's reverse engineer *again*. Take a look at your solution (if you came up with one) and the solution above. How are they different? What assumptions did you make, and how could you have eliminated them? As you can see, failing to find the answer comes down to assuming two things: first, that the woman is a shopper or customer, and second, that the items in the cart are valuable and come from the store itself. If you managed to spot this, congratulations. You might make an excellent philosopher or criminal defense lawyer!

Mystery Weight Loss

Let's play more with context—or rather, see how good we can be at *switching* between them.

The next riddle goes like this: "A man walks into a small room and presses a button. In just a few seconds, he immediately loses twenty pounds."

The question is obvious—*how on earth did he do that?*

Well, you have already been primed by this book to expect that the answer to this riddle has something to do with context. So much of life, really, doesn't make sense unless we see the full picture. Remove just a few key details of any everyday scenario and you instantly give yourself a riddle. By using global systems thinking, however, you are able to draw connections between elements and see how the whole functions as one. Or, if you only see parts of the whole, you infer and guess at the missing pieces in the same way a doctor, a detective, or perhaps even a therapist might do.

Let's try to imagine the bigger picture that could account for the curious facts we're given. Do we know of any situations in life where a person ordinarily loses twenty pounds with just the push of a button? Probably not—we'd have surely heard about it! Rather, the "losing twenty pounds" is likely a little different than we're imagining. There is an old joke where a woman's husband constantly berates her for gaining too much weight. She solves the problem by losing 160 pounds in one day— by divorcing her husband. Could a similar "losing weight" be at work here?

Or, perhaps the weight is lost only in name, in the same way as the numbers on the clock in a previous riddle don't strictly refer to actual digits or a number of items. You may have even wondered if the "pounds" was a red herring—perhaps the man enters a small gambling booth, presses a button, and immediately loses £20—the pounds here being English currency, because he's in England, because why not?

This is another riddle where most of the fun is in dreaming up potential answers—many of which could actually work. The official answer, however, is this: the small room the man enters is an elevator. When he descends to go to a lower floor, in a physical sense, he "loses" twenty pounds (and promptly gains it back again).

Driving in Circles

Have a go at the next riddle: "A woman commutes to work every day by car. When she gets to her office, however, she always drives her car round in a circle four times before parking and going inside the building. She does this every day without fail."

The question is, *why?*

Yes, the woman may be a complete nutcase. Maybe she has a weird form of OCD and has to do this ritual daily. But again, what *ordinary* context could make her behavior totally reasonable? What do we know about parking lots? It's conceivable that a person has to drive round and round a parking lot a few times before finding a spot. But it is strange that the woman drives around precisely four times before parking and entering the building, and that she always goes in circles.

Here, if you're already familiar with the unspoken context, you might have heard this riddle and have immediately seen the solution. For others who have no experience with it, the answer may be more elusive.

The answer is this: the woman works in a busy and congested part of town, and her office is on the fifth floor of an office block. To reach it, she needs to *drive up* four floors every day—resulting in her car going round and round in circles before parking.

Did you guess the answer? You may have because you could immediately conjure up this particular context. For others, however, it's not so simple. Their minds may have gotten stuck on the circles as two-dimensional ones, with the woman driving around the kind of parking lot they are more familiar with—a single-story one.

This is a very practical and obvious example of how opening the mind to consider extra dimensions can help solve a problem. We see here that the circles are not circles at all, but a connected spiral, with the extra dimension going upward and changing the picture completely. This is the same as looking at a tiny acorn and an oak tree and understanding that there is just one crucial difference between them: time.

The next time you're facing a real-world problem, be conscious of the fact that insight may be found not on the dimensions you're already aware of, but on others that you haven't considered yet. If you're struggling to make sense of some facts or ideas, try to imagine a *third* aspect that would tie them all together, rather than carrying on with what you already know (i.e. instead of trying to imagine what would compel a person to drive round a single-level parking lot four times, consider that the entire context itself could change to accommodate the seemingly strange set of facts).

A Man's Name is Called . . .

Remembering this, let's practice these skills on the following riddle. "A man hears his name spoken and is immediately taken away by two other men. Sometime later, the man dies under the care of others. What has happened to this man?"

Separately, all of these facts seem rather ordinary, but put together, they do seem a little odd. Where do the men take this man, and why do they do it only after he hears his name spoken? Does he hear anything else or just his name, and who says it? Most curiously, why does he die later, and what does it mean to say that he died under "the care of others"?

Because we already know this is a context-style riddle, let's assume that everything we've been told is in fact very ordinary and routine, if we only understand the context it occurs inside.

Can you imagine a scenario where your name would be formally and significantly spoken out loud? Perhaps at a graduation ceremony, a visa application office, or when being called to come to the reception at a doctor's office. Can you now imagine a scenario where, just after your name is spoken, you are taken away by two men? The non-negotiable nature of this taking seems to suggest either being carted off to a mental asylum against one's will or being arrested. Now, let's combine these guesses with our previous guesses to find a scenario that encompasses both. Can you picture a context where a name is called and then someone is taken away or arrested? Maybe it's coming together in your mind. Let's read the rest of the riddle to confirm our suspicions. We are told the man later dies under the care of others. Does this gel with our tentative guesses so far? Yes!

The answer to the riddle is this: the man is in a courtroom and a judge announces his verdict and officially says the man's name. The man has committed murder and is found guilty, and then sentenced to death. Later, he dies under the care of others—i.e. he is executed in custody.

The kind of thinking we use when solving such a puzzle has two uses. First, it helps us flex our imagination and creativity, dreaming up and trying out completely novel scenarios—this is the essence of problem solving. Second, it helps us gain a richer understanding of certain phenomena, insights that we might miss if we didn't understand the important role context plays.

In a murder mystery, all is revealed when we understand the *context* the crime took place in—we can suddenly see how the motive, opportunity, and means came together to produce the crime. When archeologists dig up artifacts, they only truly gain comprehension of what they are or what they were used for when they have a bigger context to plug it all into. Similarly, a therapist needs to know some back story to see the meaning behind certain feelings or actions, and a historian needs to know the particular political and cultural milieu before he can understand the writings of a person from that time. Little riddles like this seem trivial, but they help us practice a set of skills that we need in every area of life.

Surviving a Leap

Try this one on for size: "A man living in a fifty-story building decides one day to jump out of the window, but surprisingly, he survives with no injuries at all. How?"

This one will likely remind you of the window cleaner riddle we did earlier—has your brain sent you a little reminder to look for all the ways this puzzle could be solved in similar ways? Congratulations—you're learning. If you've not only tried the previous riddles but actually incorporated the lessons learned from each one, this riddle should be rather easy to complete. This is a great thing to consider: that you might have found this riddle difficult if you had never seen it before, but having practiced with a few and having "trained" your brain to do this particular kind of thinking, you can likely solve this riddle a lot faster. Isn't that amazing?

"Neuroplasticity" is the name we give to the brain's flexibility, and how we can always change and adapt the literal way our neurons are wired if we continually give our brain certain kinds of tasks to work on. If you routinely chew over difficult puzzles and riddles, your brain adapts and becomes better at doing this over time. There's a reason doctors recommend elderly people take up jigsaw puzzles, complicated card games, crosswords, and the like—just as with any muscle, the brain can atrophy when not used, but strengthen if given useful exercises.

Let's turn to the riddle again and see what we can see. If you've solved the problem already, can you see all the ways in which it's similar to the ones we've already covered? Maybe you could even make up your own riddles using the same rules. This is an exercise that really puts your brain to the task, like an engineer who takes apart a patented machine—and then understands how to build his own. Here's a related riddle that is actually a clue to this one, if you haven't figured it out yet: one man throws a deadly hand grenade at another man, who catches it in his bare hands and makes no attempt to shield himself. The man is uninjured—how?

The answer to this riddle is simply that the hand grenade was thrown with the pin still inside, so although it is strictly a deadly weapon, it's not activated. Can you use the same mental token to go back and solve the above riddle?

The answer is this: the man jumped out of a window *on the first floor*, and was naturally unharmed from leaping only a few feet.

Were you tricked by the "fifty-story building" part, assuming that a tall building is tall from every floor? Sometimes rivers are frozen, sometimes grenades are inactive, and sometimes key people in the story are not actually alive. As you encounter these strange riddles, the neurons in your brain are actually reconnecting and rewiring themselves so that the next time you face a puzzling scenario in your own life, you won't look at it in quite the same way.

A Ferocious Tiger

Our final context puzzle is not much different from the others. As always, give yourself the time to really try to figure it out before reading the answer: "A woman is slowly walking outside on a hot Sunday afternoon when she suddenly spots a ferocious tiger in the distance. Instead of immediately running away, the woman instead runs *toward* the tiger. Why?"

As always, let's begin with questions.

We know that people usually run away from tigers because they're dangerous. If this woman didn't run away, does that mean this tiger isn't dangerous? This, by the way, is a classic exercise in inference. We could then ask what circumstances might allow a tiger to no longer be dangerous. How many can you think of?

- The tiger is wounded somehow and actually needs her help, and the woman happens to be a wild animal vet

- The woman is actually hunting the tiger, and though it is dangerous, she is armed and intends to shoot it
- The tiger is incapacitated somehow, or else the woman is protected from potential attack—is she in an armored car?

Let's construct a context where a tiger is not only not dangerous, but something you might actively run toward. Have you guessed the answer yet? The solution is this: the woman is actually at a zoo, and when she sees a tiger, it's in a tiger enclosure, meaning it's not a threat to her at all. Here, a little bit of step-by-step analytical thinking helps us piece together the context where the information we see makes sense.

Takeaways:

- This chapter looks at brain teasers that make you work backward, thinking of the kind of circumstances that might make sense of the details in a question.

- A woman goes into a store and piles a shopping cart to the brim with things. She leaves the store without paying, yet nobody stops her or calls the police. Why? Think of situations where one can fill a cart with items that don't need to be paid for. The answer is trash. The woman is an employee of the store who left to throw trash in the dumpster.

- A man walks into a small room and presses a button. In a few seconds, he loses twenty pounds. How? This is another riddle where many different answers fit the criteria, but the official one is that he enters an elevator, losing twenty pounds as he descends to a lower floor.

- A man living in a fifty-story building decides to jump out of the window, but survives without sustaining any injuries. How? The fifty-story part might confuse you, but the answer is that he jumps out of a first floor window, allowing him to survive without injuring himself.

- A man hears his name spoken and is taken away by other men. Later, he dies under the care of others. What happened? Think of the context where this is possible. The answer is a courtroom, where a judge calls his name to confirm conviction. He is later executed in custody—under the care of others.
- Lastly, a woman is slowly walking outside on a hot Sunday afternoon when she spots a ferocious tiger. Instead of running away, she runs toward the tiger. Why? Think of the only time one might run toward a tiger. This can be in a zoo, where it is inside an enclosure and thus safe.

Chapter 7. Language and Word Riddles

In a sense, every riddle is a language riddle, and indeed many of the riddles we've looked at already may not translate well to other languages simply because the word tricks no longer work. The final few riddles we'll consider in this book are explicitly language-based riddles—so there's a priming clue for you already! As you read through them, try to recall how you have solved similar puzzles in the past. Remember, most importantly, that almost all riddles are not quite what they seem, and are usually solved in a wholly unexpected way. How do we get good at expecting the unexpected? That's a riddle in itself!

The Egg Riddle

Let's dive right in: "How can you drop a whole, raw egg onto a concrete floor without cracking it?"

Looks simple, huh? But luckily, you've developed an arsenal of cognitive problem-solving tricks at your disposal. You already know that it's no use to sit and think of all the hundreds of ways you could protect a fragile egg from smashing as it hits a hard floor (in fact, some of you may have even had to figure this out at school as part of science class!). For our purposes, imagine that the riddle explicitly states, "Without any padding, protection, nifty rubberized cage add-ons, or a complicated set of pulleys attached to four mini drones."

No, the solution doesn't lie there. You've already been given a clue that this is a *language-based* problem, so it probably pays to read the whole riddle again, being careful to really look at the words and how they are used. You can already guess that in all normal circumstances, an egg will crack on a hard concrete floor. Read the question again.

As it happens, this riddle is really a get-it-or-don't scenario—in other words, no amount of analytical rumination will help you see it. You either do or don't. However, it's about here in our book that we can appreciate a completely different kind of thinking. Have you ever seen a puzzle that is essentially a scrambled word like "pocateldimc" and been asked to unscramble the hidden word?

If you were to try to solve this methodically and analytically, you could start with each letter and try on every other letter as the second letter, taking the time to test out each combination possible one by one. On the other hand, you could simply look at the scrambled word without doing much of anything—just let your brain figure it out, without trying to drive the process in any way. You may be surprised to find after some looking that the word immediately springs out at you all at once.

The important thing is that your brain is working hard almost all the time, not just when you're actively engaging in some deliberate analysis, but always. For some problems, you may only need to step away and come back, to "sleep on it," or to simply ponder it without any particular direction. Let your brain do its thing.

Ready for the answer yet?

Q: How can you drop a whole, raw egg onto a concrete floor without cracking it?"

A: Concrete floors don't usually break that easily!

Ah, it was just a trick of grammar. Our preconceived models led us astray, again, although to be fair, you can be forgiven for not getting this one—it deliberately sets out to trick you. (PS, the scrambled word was "complicated"—isn't it funny how our brains make some things seem more complicated than they are?)

A Language Riddle

The next in our list goes like this: "What comes once in a minute, twice in a moment, but never in a thousand years?"

It might be useful to literally list out all the things you know about the kind of riddle you're seeing, the tools you have at your disposal to solve it, and the potential expectations that may trip you up. Slow your thought process down and really look at it. Your thought process may be something like, "Well, how could it be that a thing could happen literally every minute but not in a thousand years? That doesn't make sense. So, I guess this means that its 'coming' is not in the ordinary way I would imagine it. I also know that this chapter is about language riddles, so I'm going to go down that path and set aside an attempt to wonder what events happen on this weird schedule . . ."

As with the previous riddle and others in its category, once you see it, you see it. As a clue, try to remember what we learned earlier about being aware that *words* and the *things words refer to* are not the same thing.

If you're ready for the answer, it's this: the letter "m."

It "comes" (i.e. occurs) just once in the word minute, twice in the word moment, but not at all in the words a thousand years. There are a few riddles on this theme. For example, what word is always spelled incorrectly in the dictionary? Using the same trick we just uncovered for this riddle, you should be able to see it immediately— "incorrectly" is always spelled incorrectly!

A Wet Coat

Another cute word riddle is this one: "What kind of coat is always wet when you put it on?"

You can instantly see the kind of puzzle this is, having encountered similar ones before. Using your creative and lateral thinking, you start to think of the way the riddle is posed, your assumptions, the different possible meanings of every word in the puzzle.

Here are some clues to help you solve this (admittedly tricky) riddle:

How many kinds of "coats" can you think of? Try to list as many definitions as you can.

Of those definitions, which is wet when you put it on? The obvious one is that a coat—like a wool jacket, a blazer, or a raincoat—but none of these is always wet when you put it *on* . . .

The final clue is to consider all the different ways for someone to "put something on." If you're imagining an ordinary coat that you wear over your clothes, you might not be able to imagine any kind of coat that goes on wet. But what about the other definition for coat? Can any of those "go on wet?"

This is a clever puzzle that strengthens our ability to scan our neural networks and seek the hidden relationships that explain the connection between a series of ideas, symbols, or words. English is a language filled with homographs—words that are spelled the same but have different meanings. Add to this what we've learned about context, we can see that the key to the riddle is to find a scenario or circumstance where several different ambiguous terms are resolved. We need to find a way for one of the meanings for "coat" to fit with one of the meanings for "wet" and one of the meanings for "put on." We'll know we've found the right answer when the riddle doesn't seem mysterious anymore, but makes perfect sense!

The answer to this one is this: a coat of paint.

It is not a normal coat but a coat as in a layer, and it is not wet in the normal sense we imagine, and it is also not put on in the sense we imagine either. But you can clearly see that if the riddle had been posed to you with a little image of a jacket underneath it, this priming would have been enough to confuse you, whereas showing a little picture of a paintbrush would have alerted you to a way out of the puzzle. As always, context matters!

A Strange Law

Another short and sweet riddle goes like this: "In some states, you cannot take a picture of a man with a wooden leg. Why not?"

What on earth could be special about a man with a wooden leg, that would prohibit you from taking pictures of him? Is it even possible that a person with a wooden leg could be harmed or offended by having his photo taken, more so than a person without a wooden leg? Well, here's the clue: the previous sentences are all red herrings.

Since this is a word puzzle, we are not really interested in obscure and strange laws in some states (though they really exist, and some are a riddle unto themselves!). Rather, we need to find the answer inside the riddle itself. The egg riddle is a close cousin of this one, although this riddle has some extra details designed to lure you down the wrong path.

If you can't think of a legitimate reason why you should not be able to take a picture of a man with a wooden leg in some states when you can in others, take a moment to consider two things:

- The different meanings and connotations of the word "cannot"
- The structure of the riddle and what it's actually asking you—is there an ambiguity of phrasing there that, when identified, will reveal that you've been assuming one meaning when the riddle is assuming another?

For those who can't wait any longer to hear the answer, it's this:

Q: In some states, you cannot take a picture of a man with a wooden leg. Why not?

A: You can *never* take a picture of a man with a wooden leg in any state, or indeed a picture of a woman or anything else. That's because you can't use a wooden leg to take pictures with—you'll need a camera.

Have you ever seen a two-dimensional drawing of a cube, and simply by "flipping" your visual perspective, made the cube appear to be going into the paper or else coming out of the paper? The cube stays the same and is always two dimensional, but the way we see and interpret the marks on the page changes. This is profound—the solution is in our way of seeing and comprehending, and *not* in any innate characteristics of the phenomenon we see in front of us. We tend to think of problem solving as cleverly manipulating objects in the world, whether those objects are ideas, limitations, deadlines, etc. But it's probably more accurate to say deep problem solving occurs in the opposite way: the problem itself stays exactly as it is, and *it is we who move* and change around it, until we can see the perspective we need to.

Getting why this riddle works is like that moment when you switch perspective and the cube "pops" out of the page before your very eyes—but put your old eyes on again and the cube will go back to what it was.

The Cowboy

Our final riddle in the mental obstacle course this book has attempted to set up goes like this: "A cowboy rides into town on Friday, stays for just three nights, and then leaves on Friday—how is this possible?"

Yes, all the same word and language tricks apply here; can you spot them already?

Of course, it's one hundred percent impossible to go to a place, stay there for three nights, and then leave a week later. Let's scratch off the list any possible solutions that assume this could be achieved somehow, i.e. no faster-than-light interdimensional time travel and no funny business with parallel universes where another word for Monday is Friday.

Simply read the riddle again and again and become curious about its language and your own assumptions about the language. Here's a big clue: in what ways could Friday not be a day of the week?

You've probably guessed the answer now! Here it is: The cowboy's horse's name is Friday. He rode in on him, and he rode out on him, regardless of the days of the week.

Takeaways:

- This last set consists of language-based riddles. Focus carefully on the words used to form them.

- How can you drop a whole, raw egg onto a concrete floor without cracking it? This question deceives you into thinking of how to drop an egg without cracking it. However, the answer is that concrete floors can't be cracked using eggs!

- What comes once in a minute, twice in a moment, but never in a thousand years? Questions like these often have the solution in the question itself. The answer is the letter "m."

- What kind of coat is always wet when you put it on? The trick here is to focus on the word "coat," which doesn't refer to ordinary wearables. It refers to a coat of paint.

- In some states, you cannot take a picture of a man with a wooden leg. Why not? Like previous riddles, focus on how the riddle attempts to deceive you. Instead of wondering why picturing men with wooden legs is banned in some states, think of alternative interpretations. This reveals the answer, which is that nobody can take pictures with a wooden leg!

- Lastly, a cowboy rides into town on Friday, stays for just three nights, and then leaves on Friday. How? The key here is the word Friday, which is the name of the cowboy's horse, thus allowing him to arrive and leave on Friday.

Chapter 8. Making Sense of Riddles to Become a Better Problem Solver

Many people will hear a tricky riddle and shrug after a few minutes, demanding to know the answer. In some ways, riddles are indeed just a waste of time and a silly thing kids do, not much more sophisticated than a joke list of "1001 Animal crackers" and the like.

But in another way, riddles can show us something interesting if we can rein in our impatience and only look—not at the riddle but at *ourselves* and how we are thinking. It's difficult to maintain this strange perspective—the one in which the focus of our awareness is not the content of the problem itself but the very tools we are using. But it's essential if we are to ever learn to master and improve these skills.

Riddles may certainly seem overly simplistic on the surface, but this is a virtue if we remember that this simplicity allows us to more easily see the workings of our own minds when we approach such riddles. Sometimes, it takes something seemingly simple and obvious to show us what is actually rather complicated.

Having gone through the riddles in this book, you've likely developed your own set of mental schemas, models, and intellectual tools along the way. These are all transferrable skills—if we make the effort to transfer them! Before we conclude this book, let's consider not only the concrete tools we've developed, but practical ways we can use these skills in "real life," with problems and puzzles you're likely to encounter every day.

A List of all the Right Questions . . .

If you care about a problem or tricky situation, take the time to unravel and analyze it carefully bit by bit. Don't assume your brain will always run off and solve it correctly by itself. It may, or you may simply default to bias and lazy habitual thinking, never truly innovating, and never really moving beyond your own conceptual limitations. Whether your problem is a professional, personal, physical, financial, or relational one, the following questions can help activate the skills you've learned in this book to more deliberately and consciously solve them. By slowing down, deliberately recruiting our mental tools, and giving ourselves the time to arrive at a considered solution, we make better choices and work our way through difficulties faster. Here are the questions:

- Am I seeing all the information here? What do I not know, and most importantly, can I start to even think of the things I don't even know I don't know? This constitutes a blind spot, and these are dangerous because you could be running in the opposite direction for all you know. A lay of the land is important first and foremost.

- Can I list out my assumptions about this scenario, and then check whether I actually have evidence for each one? How could I find information to fill in these gaps rather than just assuming I already know? This is a question that takes you out of the big picture and forces you to start thinking in smaller steps.

- Does this problem look like anything I've encountered before? If so, can the solution I used then be used here? Maybe with some adaptations? What kind of past experiences can I draw upon, and how can I also make sure that I don't get trapped in those same experiences?

- Let's imagine I did find a solution—what would it look like? What form would it take, and what mindset would I likely need to have to discover it?

- Can I lay out the premises of the argument I'm looking at? Can I see the logic in the arguments, or is there a flaw that I've overlooked? How can I verify this and ensure that I am not being motivated by something other than a pursuit of the truth?

- Is it possible that I'm completely off the mark here? Have I debated myself and gone through the thought exercise of trying to prove myself wrong in order to confirm matters?

- How many ways can I change my perspective, my attitude, or my focus to see this circumstance differently? Can I imagine the viewpoint of someone else, or a different context that helps me better understand this situation? Whose perspective can I borrow?

- What are my expectations here, and are they warranted?

- Are the tools that I'm using—my models, theories, or ideas—actually a good fit for my situation? Could it be that the problem is in the tools I'm using? Do I need to take a step back to consider what my true goal is again?

- Can I ask better questions here? Even if they're a bit "out there"? Do I need to think outside the box and look in non-obvious places?

- Can I zoom out and look at the bigger picture? What are other people's motivations, what is the history of this scenario, and what are the contextual clues that will help me see this problem as a whole rather than just a single phenomenon?
- What is the quality of the information I've gathered? Is it enough? Is it actually true? Are the sources good? What happens when I deliberately seek out information that goes against what I currently believe?
- Could I take a step back, "sleep on it," and return to the problem later?
- Is there even a problem at all, or does it just appear to be one because of the perspective I'm taking?
- What other dimensions could I understand this problem via? How will the situation evolve over time, for example, or what are some other causes and effects I haven't considered?
- Do I need to do more research, or have I actually done too much already?
- Can I look again at all those avenues of enquiry or potential solutions that I've

written off because they're "impossible" or don't make sense (yet)?

- How am I using language and symbolism here? Have I mistaken the symbol for something as the thing itself? What happens when I play around with the words or symbols I assign to things?
- Considering mistakes I have made in this area in the past, what do I already know about how *not* to do things?
- How would a completely different person solve this problem?
- Is the area of the problem I'm considering really the most relevant area, or have I gotten distracted?
- Can I just look at this problem without trying to solve it for a second, just with curiosity and the willingness to see it as clearly as I can (knowing that sometimes wanting a particular kind of answer is an expectation and bias in itself)?
- Where can I find help, and who can I ask?
- Have I asked enough "what if" questions? What do the answers tell me?
- Finally, what would my decision process or thinking look like if I removed my ego

completely, or if I wasn't afraid of being wrong?

Becoming a better problem solver and critical thinker is not about being *right*. If anything, it's about finding better and better ways to be wrong! It's far better to "fail" at a task and learn something valuable along the way than to easily understand something right off the bat and never truly know why or how to replicate the process. So, don't be in too much of a hurry to become a masterful, intelligent thinking machine who vanquishes every problem that emerges! Instead of committing to solving problems, commit to developing the best set of attitudes and critical/analytical skills as you possibly can. In this, you can always be "right."

"Riddle-Thinking" Applied

Example 1

Problem solving in the real world often cannot be done through simply analyzing information or facts as they are given to you. Companies often face this issue when trying to market their products to an international audience consisting of different cultures. Multinational chains like Starbucks, McDonalds, and KFC often fail to break into specific countries and expand as successfully as they have in the US or western Europe. The following example illustrates how "riddle-thinking" can help companies be more astute.

Imagine a CEO who invests a lot of money into marketing his product internationally, having found immense success locally. He finds the best translators, marketers, and distributors to get the product launched in several countries abroad. Out of four new markets, all do well except one—where the product flops spectacularly and he loses money. He has to figure out why and fix the issue soon or consider withdrawing his presence, as it's simply costing too much.

The team at the company's headquarters mull over the reasons it failed. They look at everything they can think of—the local economy, the price point, the market in general, even the political and cultural climate in the country in question. They find nothing to explain the dismal sales. They run through a list of questions much like the one in the previous section, and soon realize there's something big they're not seeing. It's a real riddle!

The problem persisted until the CEO heads to the country himself to see what's up. Within just a few moments of being in a store that sells his product, he spots the problem. The color of the package design closely matches another completely unrelated product in the store—a muddle that has rather embarrassing connotations for his own product. By being literally in the store that his potential customer is in (i.e. the context), he sees the problem—people are mistaking his product for something else. He goes home, completely changes the design of the product, and soon sees sales pick up in that country.

In this case, no amount of analyzing and mulling over potential strategies would have helped the CEO or his team realize what the problem was. Nor is it possible for them to account for each and every factor that influences the success or failure of a product in a given market.

Ultimately, it turned out that the problem was never with the product itself, but the way it was being perceived due to its similarity to another product. The CEO utilized some divergent thinking to try to account for more localized factors by visiting the country where his product had failed. Since his product succeeded in three of the four markets he had launched it in, he could probably infer that the product itself was not the issue. Instead, it had to be something restricted to the one place where it failed, and the CEO turned out to be right.

Steve Jobs used fairly similar tactics when he was first trying to promote the MacBook.

Knowing how laptops are displayed in stores everywhere, placed in a line on display one beside the other, he was keenly aware that the MacBook would be perceived as just another laptop when placed alongside others. Sitting beside a Dell or an HP laptop would undermine the fact that it ran on a software that was completely different, among other novel features.

To solve the issue, he came up with the idea of having a separate section for Apple laptops to help it stand out from its competitors. This eventually resulted in Apple deciding to run their own stores in the US and, later, worldwide. Just like the CEO in the example, Jobs put himself in the shoes of his customers and simulated their experience while buying a product to enhance the way it is perceived in the market. If we go back to the steps laid out in chapter one, this enabled the CEO to implement step two, which was research more effectively since he now has the relevant information that he did not previously possess. This, in turn, helped him solve the problem.

Example 2

A certain much-loved cheese is usually made traditionally, but manufacturers are increasingly producing it in factories. A company decides to scan the country for

local artisans to find out more about their recipes and techniques, so they can replicate them in their own massive industrial kitchens. An engineer looks at a farm cheese industry and notices the many steps it takes to make the cheese. He also notices that the farmer spends considerable time running back and forth with trays of milk and curds at varying stages of the cheese-making process. The engineer makes a note of the process and technique and knows that he can build a more efficient factory setup that removes the need to run back and forward between sections of the kitchen or carry trays.

He designs a complex cheese factory mechanism that speeds up the process. The company excitedly awaits the day when they start producing this delicacy on a larger, more profitable scale. And then one day, the cheese is ready . . . and it's terrible. Nobody can figure out what's wrong. All the right ingredients have been used (even better ones!) and the techniques followed with machine-like accuracy. After spending all this money, the company soon realizes they didn't grasp the totality of the cheese-making process as well as they thought. What did they miss? It's a real riddle. What else goes into cheese making that they didn't include in their ultra-modern and sophisticated factory process?

They keep asking this question and keep getting the same answer: nothing. They did everything correctly and ultra-efficiently. The engineer looks again at his

assumptions. Could the problem actually lie in the solution itself? He goes back to the cheese farm and looks again and suddenly understands. By dawdling and

running back and forth with trays of curds and milk, the farmer actually gave the

cheese vital cooling time between steps of the process, resulting in a better, more

delicate flavor—something the factory design completely eliminated because the engineer labeled this part of the process "inefficient."

Instead of looking to find what was wrong with the factory, he used riddle-like thinking and asked, could it be that the factory is too efficient? The engineer was able to see that his assumptions were unfounded. What he thought was simple inefficiency was in fact a vital part of the cheese-making process. He neglected this because his main goal was to speed up the process of producing cheese. Unable to account for any logical reason the farmer would spend so much time running back and forth with the trays, he simply concludes there isn't one.

This is a mistake we are often prone to making in real life, but it is important to remember that the inability to rationalize something just requires a different approach.

Ultimately, after exhausting all explanations, he was forced to go back to the traditional method of making cheese to identify the factor he had missed. However, he might never have found the source of the problem unless he took the time to question a very fundamental premise, i.e. "the way we are doing this is obviously right." When faced with a seemingly intractable issue, it isn't always easy to admit that maybe our approach is wrong. However, recognizing mistakes is part of the process of learning, and the engineer only realized his mistake after admitting defeat.

All it took was challenging all the assumptions he had made in the process of designing his modernized factory.

Sherlock Holmes, the famous detective from Arthur Conan Doyle's stories, frequently succeeds in solving the most complex mysteries due to this simple tactic. He rarely assumes anything, and keeps his mind open to all sorts of possibilities, ones that others unconsciously reject or do not even consider. He then uses these possibilities to form a chain of inferences that usually helps him perform the logical gymnastics his fans have come to love.

As the engineer was to discover, even one assumption can break the entire process. Technically, he did not make any errors in replicating the process itself, as he followed each step meticulously as the farmers did. Yet, his cheese came up short because it missed a key ingredient that the traditional method did not dispense with: time.

It is not clear that even the farmer is aware of this being a key ingredient of his cheese. He might not be carrying the trays back and forth repeatedly due to an awareness of its benefits, but simply the fact that the process ultimately produces great cheese. If the engineer had utilized his systems thinking more perceptively and tried to account for how each component of the cheese-making process contributes to its flavor, he might have saved himself much time and resources.

Example 3

Zookeepers have purchased a new and exotic pair of animals that they hope to breed with. The animals arrive, and everyone excitedly waits to see the results of their breeding program. But after years and years, the couple produce no offspring. The zookeepers research the animal in exhaustive depth. They do whatever they can to facilitate the process, and can't understand what they're doing wrong. Everything is perfect, and yet the pair won't breed! In fact, the animals could often be observed fighting with one another despite the best efforts of everyone involved.

Eventually, a renowned animal expert comes to visit and sees the problem in a heartbeat—the zoo has mistakenly been trying to mate two females. In seeking ever more complicated solutions to get offspring from their breeding pair, the zookeepers have missed one crucial factor—they don't have a breeding pair! This example is very similar to a real-life incident that occurred in northern Japan, wherein zookeepers spent years trying to breed two hyenas that ultimately turned out to be both male. They had been given the hyenas as a male and female couple, and did not think to question that until faced with their failure to breed them.

In both cases, the mistake was the very first step that the zookeepers took—forming the pairs of animals for breeding. Yet, when they tried to solve the problem, they never questioned this very foundational premise that they had long assumed to be true. It wasn't the animals that were somehow failing to reproduce; they couldn't possibly as a matter of biological fact.

Instead, the zookeepers had, going back to the steps in chapter one, failed to identify the specifics of their problem. As such, any future steps, like researching and identifying biases, were doomed to failure. Like in the previous example, the path to finding the right solution begins by accepting one's own mistakes. This is how the engineer and zookeepers both recognize their faulty assumptions, and are ultimately able to rectify them.

One important distinction between this example and the previous one is the fact that in the latter, the engineer himself makes a wrong assumption. However, here, the zookeepers are given information by someone in authority that they unconsciously take to be true. This makes it much harder to spot the problem, since it did not originate in the thinking of the zookeepers themselves. While the engineer doubted the farmer, the zookeepers trusted the animal supplier, yet both are problematic in their respective circumstances.

The next time you face some annoying, puzzling, seemingly impossible scenario in your own life, pause for a moment. Can you approach it like a game, a riddle, or a simple brain teaser? Some of the problems we encounter in life have enormously high stakes, but their underlying mechanisms may ultimately be no more complex than the "tricks" you've identified in the riddles above. Many businessmen, leaders, great thinkers, artists, and scientists have had extraordinary Eureka moments not by staying within their own conceptual frameworks, but in stepping momentarily outside them. The previous chapters outline the various ways of thinking they utilize to do so, and it is up to you to figure out which one suits your circumstances the best.

We can all learn different skills, different languages, and so on to succeed in life. But the most fundamental skills of all is the ability to think, to learn, to adapt, and to think about your own thinking. Do this, and any skill set is open to you. Better yet, you have the conceptual vocabulary to appraise your own processes, make adjustments, and improve.

As was mentioned before, we rarely think about the way we think. This process, called metacognition, is the key to avoid falling into logical traps, thinking lazily, or missing relevant information that is often staring us in the face. The best way to avoid this is to debate with yourself and challenge the conclusions you arrive at. This will help train your mind to consider all possibilities in any given situation, allowing you to see things more clearly and make correct inferences from the information available to you.

Takeaways:

- Though riddles are often framed in relatively simple words, they can be incredibly complex, utilizing many different but important modes of thinking.

- When faced with a tricky problem, asking yourself the right questions can often be the key to solving them. These include analyzing whether you've identified the problem correctly, what a solution might look like, whether the tools you're using to solve the issue are actually correct, etc.

- The type of thinking that riddles utilize can be very useful when applied in real life. For example, a CEO launches his product in four countries, and it succeeds in three of them. Despite spending enormous resources, neither he nor his team can figure out why the product failed in one country. To find out, the CEO visits this country to help him contextualize the problem more accurately. When he visits the shop selling his product, he recognizes the issue—its package design is similar to another product that carries embarrassing connotations. Thus, some divergent thinking helped him solve his problem.

- Here is another example. An engineer wishes to replicate traditionally made cheese for production in factories. He observes the process and reduces the time taken to produce cheese as much as he can. However, his factory-produced cheese turns out to be terrible. In examining his process, the engineer discovers the problem. He had wrongly assumed one part of the traditional process to be an inefficiency, even though it turned out to be vital. Riddle-thinking helped him identify the fallacy of his assumptions.

- Finally, consider that zookeepers once spent much resources and time trying to mate two animals, only to find out that both animals in the pair were female. How did they end up making this error? Like in the previous example, they assumed something that wasn't true. Riddle-thinking helps counter this sort of lazy thinking, enabling one to make more logically sound deductions.

Summary Guide

Chapter 1. "I'm a Puzzle that Everyone Loves not Being Able to Solve—What Am I?"

- Riddles are phrases or questions framed in the form of puzzles that require all types of thinking to deduce its answer or some double meaning underlying its words. They employ several different patterns of thinking, challenging us to work with limited information in unique ways. No one style of thinking is better than the other. Each is useful in different situations, and we must grasp how to apply them correctly. This is exactly what riddles help us learn, since it involves many different thinking styles.

- The most important tool that helps solve riddles is divergent thinking. This form of thinking demands that you survey and analyze all possible solutions to any given problem. In its opposite, convergent (or critical) thinking, we generally operate within a set of rules and use them to work our way to arrive at answers. However, in divergent thinking, the rules are immaterial, and we must explore any and all relevant solutions.

- Other important tools include lateral thinking, which involves studying how we infer something from information given to us. Systems thinking calls on you to look at the bigger picture, namely how components of any idea or solution fit with one another to form a coherent whole. Lastly, inspirational thinking requires you to gain insight from some source, like a peak experience or an altered state of consciousness. This type of thinking lets our unconscious mind solve problems for us, allowing our conscious selves to benefit from it.

- A complete problem-solving strategy involves a certain sequence that combines all of these thinking frameworks. Often, the first step is to identify the specifics of the problem you're faced with. Following that, you need to evaluate the quality of the information available through research. Identify any biases you may have, and debate with yourself to recognize any holes in your logic.

Chapter 2. Situational Riddles

- Situational riddles are those that involve some bizarre circumstances that have taken place. Your job is to account for or explain why the situation materialized in that particular way by challenging assumptions one commonly holds. The lowest hanging fruit in terms of solutions or reasoning almost never applies, so it's up to you to deduce what's really going on.

- Imagine a man who walks into a bar and asks the bartender for a glass of water. The bartender instead brings out a firearm and points it at the man, who then promptly thanks him and leaves immediately. What happened here?

- Think about why the man asked for water, why he was offered a gunshot instead, and why he would thank the bartender for it. What use could water and a gun have in common? The answer is to get rid of hiccups. The fear of a gunshot chased the man's hiccups away just like a glass of water would.

- A man in an open field lies dead with an unopened package next to him. No animal or human is around him. How did he die?

- Think of the sorts of packages that can cause death without being opened. Using divergent thinking, we can deduce that one type of package is a parachute. The man had jumped out a plane and died because his parachute did not open.

- A woman gives birth to two sons born in the same hour of the same day. But they aren't twins. How? The key here is to think of how one can have two babies without being twins. There is a slight omission of information here. The simple answer is that they are triplets.

- Finally, a woman shoots her husband, then holds him underwater for five minutes. Later, they go out for dinner and have a nice time. What happened? Come up with non-lethal ways one can shoot someone and hold them underwater. Again, we have wordplay here. You'll eventually arrive at photography. The woman is a photographer shooting her husband with a camera. Holding him underwater is really his photo in developing solution.

Chapter 3. More Complex Analytical Riddles

- Analytical riddles are more challenging than situational ones because instead of shifting perspectives, they require you to carefully analyze information to arrive at conclusions. This is the classic comparison of divergent versus convergent thinking. It might be easier depending on your proclivities, but often, the devil is in the details.
- Five men are walking together when it starts to rain. Four of them start walking quickly, while the fifth doesn't. Yet he stays dry, and the other four get wet. They all arrive at their destination at the same time. How?
- Logically examining the details reveals the answer, the fifth man was dead and being carried in a coffin by the other four. This is how he did not get wet, didn't pick up pace, and yet reached his destination at the same time as the others. This was some kind of funeral situation.

- A window cleaner is cleaning windows on the twenty-fifth floor of a skyscraper when he slips and falls, yet isn't harmed despite not wearing any safety equipment. How?

- It is easy to fall into the trap of thinking of ways one can fall twenty-five floors without dying, but the answer here is that he never does. He was cleaning the windows from inside the building.

- Two girls order iced teas at a restaurant. The first girl drinks hers quickly and orders four more, while the other drinks her first one slowly. The teas were poisoned, but only the second girl dies. How?

- Think of the ingredients in iced tea: ice and tea. This reveals the solution, wherein the ice was poisoned. Thus, the second girl dies because her ice has more time to melt, whereas the first girl escapes this by drinking her tea quickly.

- Finally, what disappears the moment you say its name? Think of what the opposite is to saying something aloud. It's silence, which is what disappears when you say something.

Chapter 4. Brain Teasers

- The following set of riddles exploits the cognitive shortcuts and assumptions our brain makes.
- You are in a dark cabin and you have a single match in a matchbox, a candle, a newspaper, and an oil stove. Which do you light first?
- The answer is to light the match first. We generally disregard the match and focus on the other three options, yet the match is the obvious and correct answer.
- What five-letter word becomes shorter when you add two letters to it? Seemingly contradictory, the answer is the word short, where adding e and r makes it "shorter." These types of riddles often include the solution within the question itself.

- How can you add two to eleven and get one as the correct answer? This riddle appears to be mathematically impossible, since 11+2 cannot equal 1. However, the context matters. Adding two hours to 11 o'clock yields 1 o'clock, which is the correct answer.

- What makes more as you take them? There can be multiple correct answers to this one, as long as the object fulfils the condition that it increases the more we take it. Photographs and footsteps are both examples of this.

- A man takes his car to a big hotel, and the moment he arrives there, he is instantly declared bankrupt. Why? Again, analyze the context. In what world does arriving at a hotel cause bankruptcy? The answer is Monopoly, where the car piece is the man's token, and arriving at a hotel results in bankruptcy.

Chapter 5. More Classic Brain Teasers

- This chapter contains more riddles that challenge normal ways of thinking.
- I don't have a voice, but I speak to you. I tell you all the things that people in the world do. I have leaves, but I'm not a tree; I have a spine but am not human. I have hinges but am not a door. What am I?
- Think of something that has leaves, spines, and hinges. Bibliophiles will recognize that the answer is a book. Through its words, it "speaks" without having a voice, its pages are leaves, and the binding forms its spine and hinges.
- Next, a man and his dog are on opposite sides of a river. The man calls his dog, who immediately crosses the river without a bridge, boat, or any other assistance. He also crosses over without getting wet. How? Focus on the river. What type of river can be crossed without

getting wet, or without a bridge or boat? The answer is a frozen one.

- A man is out walking when it begins to rain. He's in the middle of nowhere, with nowhere to hide and nothing to cover himself with. He arrives home completely soaked, but not a single hair on his head is wet. How? Is there a way a man can be soaked without a single hair on his head being wet? This can only be possible if the man is bald, which is the right answer.

- Paul is an assistant at a butcher's shop. He is a little over six feet tall and wears a size nine shoe. What does Paul weigh? The last line might trick you into trying to deduce Paul's weight, but the answer is he weighs meat, because he is a butcher's assistant!

- The person who makes it has no need for it. The person who buys it doesn't use it, and the person who uses it doesn't know why they are using it. What is it? An obvious answer might be a baby crib, but the official one is a coffin.

Chapter 6. Context Riddles

- This chapter looks at brain teasers that make you work backward, thinking of the kind of circumstances that might make sense of the details in a question.
- A woman goes into a store and piles a shopping cart to the brim with things. She leaves the store without paying, yet nobody stops her or calls the police. Why? Think of situations where one can fill a cart with items that don't need to be paid for. The answer is trash. The woman is an employee of the store who left to throw trash in the dumpster.
- A man walks into a small room and presses a button. In a few seconds, he loses twenty pounds. How? This is another riddle where many different answers fit the criteria, but the official one is that he enters an

elevator, losing twenty pounds as he descends to a lower floor.

- A man living in a fifty-story building decides to jump out of the window, but survives without sustaining any injuries. How? The fifty-story part might confuse you, but the answer is that he jumps out of a first floor window, allowing him to survive without injuring himself.

- A man hears his name spoken and is taken away by other men. Later, he dies under the care of others. What happened? Think of the context where this is possible. The answer is a courtroom, where a judge calls his name to confirm conviction. He is later executed in custody—under the care of others.

- Lastly, a woman is slowly walking outside on a hot Sunday afternoon when she spots a ferocious tiger. Instead of running away, she runs toward the tiger. Why? Think of the only time one might run toward a tiger. This can be in a zoo, where it is inside an enclosure and thus safe.

Chapter 7. Language and Word Riddles

- This last set consists of language-based riddles. Focus carefully on the words used to form them.

- How can you drop a whole, raw egg onto a concrete floor without cracking it? This question deceives you into thinking of how to drop an egg without cracking it. However, the answer is that concrete floors can't be cracked using eggs!

- What comes once in a minute, twice in a moment, but never in a thousand years? Questions like these often have the solution in the question itself. The answer is the letter "m."

- What kind of coat is always wet when you put it on? The trick here is to focus on the word "coat," which doesn't refer to ordinary wearables. It refers to a coat of paint.

- In some states, you cannot take a picture of a man with a wooden leg. Why not? Like previous riddles, focus on how the riddle attempts to deceive you. Instead of wondering why picturing men with wooden legs is banned in some states, think of alternative interpretations. This reveals the answer, which is that nobody can take pictures with a wooden leg!

- Lastly, a cowboy rides into town on Friday, stays for just three nights, and then leaves on Friday. How? The key here is the word Friday, which is the name of the cowboy's horse, thus allowing him to arrive and leave on Friday.

Chapter 8. Making Sense of Riddles to Become a Better Problem Solver

- Though riddles are often framed in relatively simple words, they can be incredibly complex, utilizing many different but important modes of thinking.
- When faced with a tricky problem, asking yourself the right questions can often be the key to solving them.

These include analyzing whether you've identified the problem correctly, what a solution might look like, whether the tools you're using to solve the issue are actually correct, etc.

- The type of thinking that riddles utilize can be very useful when applied in real life. For example, a CEO launches his product in four countries, and it succeeds in three of them. Despite spending enormous resources, neither he nor his team can figure out why the product failed in one country. To find out, the CEO visits this country to help him contextualize the problem more accurately. When he visits the shop selling his product, he recognizes the issue—its package design is similar to another product that carries embarrassing connotations. Thus, some divergent thinking helped him solve his problem.

- Here is another example. An engineer wishes to replicate traditionally made cheese for production in factories. He observes the process and reduces the time taken to produce cheese as much as he can. However, his factory-produced cheese turns out to be terrible. In examining his process, the engineer discovers the problem. He had wrongly assumed one part of the traditional process to be an inefficiency, even though it turned out to be vital. Riddle-thinking helped him identify the fallacy of his assumptions.

- Finally, consider that zookeepers once spent much resources and time trying to mate two animals, only to find out that both animals in the pair were female. How did they end up making this error? Like in the previous example, they assumed something that wasn't true. Riddle-thinking helps counter this sort of lazy thinking, enabling one to make more logically sound deductions.